Robinson Township Library
Robinson, Illinois 62454

364.1   41559
Cox
Cox, Robert V.
Missing person.

Robinson Township Library
Robinson, Illinois 62454

Missing Person

MISSING PERSON

Robert V. Cox

and

Kenneth L. Peiffer, Jr.

STACKPOLE BOOKS

Copyright © 1979 by Robert V. Cox and Kenneth L. Peiffer, Jr.

Published by
STACKPOLE BOOKS
Cameron and Kelker Streets
P.O. Box 1831
Harrisburg, Pa. 17105

Published simultaneously in Don Mills, Ontario, Canada
by Thomas Nelson & Sons, Ltd.

Some of the names of the people involved in the story have been changed to protect the innocent. However, all events are factual.

All rights reserved, including the right to reproduce this book or portions thereof in any form or by any means, electronic or mechanical, including photocopying, recording, or by any information storage and retrieval system, without permission in writing from the publisher. All inquiries should be addressed to Stackpole Books, Cameron and Kelker Streets, P.O. Box 1831, Harrisburg, Pennsylvania 17105.

Library of Congress Cataloging in Publication Data

Cox, Robert V   1927–
   Missing person.

    1. Parapsychology and criminal investigation—Case studies. 2. Kline, Deborah Sue. 3. Allison, Dorothy.
I. Peiffer, Kenneth L., joint author. II. Title.
BF1045.C7C68 1978   364.1'54'0974844   78-12024
ISBN 0-8117-1002-5

Printed in the U.S.A.

To the memory of Debbie Kline

Contents

Authors' Preface   13

Part 1

THE DISAPPEARANCE

    ONE   17
    July 22, 1976

    TWO   21
    6:45 P.M.

    THREE   31
    Saturday, July 24

    FOUR   37
    The First Week

FIVE   45
The Second Week

SIX   55
Dead Ends

Part 2

SUSPICION

ONE   69
Beauty and the Beast

TWO   81
December 1976

THREE   87
At the Bingaman Farm

FOUR   93
December 1976
Waynesboro, Pennsylvania

FIVE   97
Leave-taking, September 1976

SIX   101
A Reluctant Convert

SEVEN   105
The First Clue

EIGHT   111
The Undercover Agent

NINE   117
The Source

Acknowledgments

Our sincere thanks to Lynn Harnett, Rodman Philbrick, and Frank Coffey for their skilled and important editorial assistance.

We also wish to acknowledge the following persons without whom MISSING PERSON could not have been written: Cpl. John Sabric, Tpr. Kenton Paul, Tpr. Cordes Chambers, Tpr. Randy Kepner, Cpl. Robert Kissner, Tpr. Joe Claycomb, Jim Rumberger, Ken Horn, Bobby Nye, Betty Wingert, Jesse Garber, Virginia Wishard, David Lively, Sid Miller, and John S. Snyder Jr.

Authors' Preface

We are a team: We worked together to find out the story behind the story. We started *Missing Person* from the beginning and stayed with it to the end. In order to bring you the most accurate and unbiased account of Debbie Kline's disappearance, the ensuing investigation, and the startling climax, we have placed ourselves in the third person to maintain our objectivity.

We, like the majority of law-enforcement personnel, entered the story with a common thought: a young girl was having a fling and would return to her family in a few days.

But we were convinced within a short time, as were police investigators, that our first impressions were wrong. The sincerity of the Kline family satisfied us that this was not a conventional case.

To her parents, relatives, and friends, Debbie was more than just a statistic. She was a most unlikely prospect to join the ranks of "missing persons."

And we never dreamed at the beginning just how unconventional the case would become before it was solved. Our relationships with police, Debbie's family, and the many others who helped solve the case, especially Dorothy Allison, provided this inside story of those involved.

Here, then, in the words of everyone who lived through the ordeal, is *Missing Person.*

Robert V. Cox
Kenneth L. Peiffer, Jr.

Part 1

THE
DISAPPEARANCE

ONE

July 22, 1976

Debbie Kline was radiant that summer afternoon. The whole marvelous world seemed to stretch before her. As she polished the last piece of stainless steel at the Waynesboro Hospital cafeteria, she thought again of her first paycheck. Her thoughts raced back over the last few weeks, which had in many ways been tumultuous, even exhilirating. Scarcely a month had passed since high-school graduation, but already she had a brand-new car and a full-time job. Debbie also had plans—she intended to save money so that she could travel and see some of the world—but that evening she wanted to celebrate by taking her parents out to dinner.

After she'd buffed and polished the last countertop, Debbie glanced up at the clock. Moments later she left the building, walking with a spring in her step. The afternoon heat pressed around her, and it rose, shimmering, across the asphalt parking lot. Her heart leaped as she spied her new Vega. Its burgundy sheen glowed in the rising heat. But the car was no mirage. She recalled the day she had picked it out. Her father had stood beside it, looking taller than ever as he remarked on its attractive color. Her mother had beamed with quiet pride.

Debbie strode purposefully across the lot and unlocked the car door. She was looking forward to the breezy ride home as she rolled down the driver's side window. Adjusting the rearview mirror, Debbie examined her face. It looked, she playfully reassured herself, much more mature than the one she had seen in last month's mirror.

She clicked open her wallet and looked again at her paycheck.

Pay to the bearer... Deborah Sue Kline... $136.00. It meant she had gained acceptance into the adult world. So engrossed was she in these thoughts that Debbie never noticed the indulgent smile of affection that beamed from the face of a passing coworker.

The Vega started instantly. Before readjusting the rearview mirror, she freed her long, honey-colored hair from the tight bun she wore at work. Then, tapping her fingers in rhythm to a melody that was running through her head, she drove onto the main road.

Debbie was mentally dividing her paycheck. Some would be set aside for the Vega, some would go into her savings account, but the best portion, if not the largest, would be happily spent that evening. Her thoughts turned to the selection of the restaurant where she would treat her parents to dinner.

She checked the mirror with conscientious frequency, noting that several cars were behind her. After she had passed through the small-town, rush-hour bustle of Waynesboro, only one car remained—the dark green Cougar that had been behind her since she left the hospital parking lot.

The wind blew back her thick, naturally wavy hair. She took

a deep breath of the fresh air, reveling in the ride home. On either side were fields green with corn, the thick wooded areas, and the homes of people she had known for most of her life.

Debbie saw ahead of her the charred remains of the Reverend Moyer's new home. She shook her head at the sight of the lone chimney, standing upright forlornly through the rubble. It seemed such a senseless waste.

Suddenly the Cougar spun out from its place behind her, spitting gravel. Startled, she glanced left. Her eyes widened as she met the stares of two men.

One of the men grinned.

TWO

6:45 P.M.

On that long, warm evening there was still plenty of light in the sky. And the light had that rich summer quality that Jane Kline so appreciated. She loved the mild Pennsylvania summers, when life moved slowly, and with dignity. The view from her front porch did not resemble the frantic world she saw on the evening news. Not much happened in the sleepy little town of Waynesboro, and Jane preferred it that way.

The steady drone of a small engine soothed her. Dick, her husband of twenty-six years, was mowing the lawn. She glanced at the clock, then walked to the front porch and called him.

"Dick, it's a quarter to seven. Do you think Debbie could have had trouble with her car?"

Dick Kline, a tall, ruggedly built man with sandy hair, was the superintendent of the Waynesboro Country Club, and he was used to arduous outdoor work. As he looked up at his wife, he smiled, then shrugged. The lawn mower seemed dwarfed by his enormous forearms and massive chest.

"Might have had a flat, I suppose. But she's only a few minutes late. Let me finish up this corner of the lawn and if she isn't home by then, we'll go have a look."

Dick wasn't worried. The Vega was brand new and Debbie was a careful driver. Kline considered himself a lucky man. He had a home of his own, a loving wife, and six fine children. Deborah Sue, third eldest, was, in his eyes, as near to perfect as a daughter could be. He recalled her delight when he and Jane agreed to help her buy a new car. And then she'd gone out immediately and gotten a full-time job to help pay for it. At eighteen she had a fully developed sense of responsibility, and he was proud of that. He knew from stories he'd heard that many of the other girls her age were more inclined to mischief than to responsibility.

As he put away the lawn mower he was hoping she hadn't had trouble with the car. She would be terribly disappointed if the Vega turned out to be a lemon.

"Could she have stopped off somewhere?" he asked his wife as they backed out of the driveway. Jane looked worried.

"I don't think so," she said. "She got paid today and she was going to take us out to dinner."

Dick nodded. It was just past seven o'clock, and he fully expected to meet his daughter coming the other way. Debbie would be apologetic, he knew, for she prided herself on being punctual. With that in mind he began retracing the route she would have taken home.

The Klines drove past the pond next to the Fish and Game clubhouse. A few swimmers were still there, splashing around in the cool water. Dick banked the big Chevy around the sharp curve. Glancing to his left, he saw the burned-out Moyer house. Heavy underbrush and dense trees obscured the view of the pile of debris that only a week ago had been a beautiful home. Now all that remained standing was a small wooden toolshed along the edge of the road and the chimney thrusting up through charred timbers.

The sky was just beginning to darken, and the occasional flash of a firefly could be seen in the rolling fields. The hot tar of the macadam road sounded sticky under the tires. Jane and Dick Kline passed by the homes and farms that flanked the road the rest of the way into town. As they entered the Waynesboro Hospital parking lot, Jane craned her neck, hoping to catch sight of her daughter. There was no sign of Debbie.

Her parents were now concerned. They decided to cover a larger area before retracing their path. Perhaps Debbie had run a last-minute errand that took her beyond her usual route home. Perhaps her car had broken down on a back road.

Perhaps she'd had an accident.

Harold Gingrich, chief of police, swung out of his cruiser and strode toward the toolshed at the Moyer property. The sight of the burned ruins angered him. He didn't like to think there was an arsonist in the area, and the fire chief had assured him that the blaze was deliberately set.

Behind the woodshed Gingrich found the dark-colored car, just as it had been reported. It had been pushed or driven deep into the bushes, as though to hide it, and he wondered if the abandoned car was in any way connected to the fire. He noted the license-plate numbers and then leaned in to have a look at the interior.

"Maybe she's back home by now. It's possible we passed her," said Dick, trying to calm his wife. "The light plays funny tricks this time of day."

Jane Kline shook her head. She sensed that something was wrong, terribly wrong.

"Look!" she cried.

Dick jammed on the brakes instinctively. Blue lights were flashing from the Moyer place, and as he slowed he caught sight of a dark compact car. Casting a furtive glance at his wife, he backed quickly into the driveway.

It was Debbie's car.

Jane leaped out of the car before her husband had a chance to turn off the ignition. She ran toward Chief Gingrich with one thought in her mind.

"That's my daughter's car! Where is she?" she cried. Dick's long legs enabled him to catch up with her before the policeman had a chance to reply.

"I don't know. Just got here myself and radioed for a license check. You say this is your daughter's car? Nobody around when I got here, ma'am. But she left in a hurry, because the driver's side door is open, the window is down, and the keys are in the ignition."

He looked directly at the couple and noticed that they both appeared to be horrified by his mild statement. Jane Kline peered into the car as though she might find her daughter there, somehow overlooked by the policeman.

"The car was just as you see it now," Chief Gingrich continued. "It looks like it might have been pushed into that little tree."

He moved around to the front of the vehicle and noted the spot where the front bumper had made an imprint on the bark. He had already determined that the interior of the car was spotless, still exuding the odor peculiar to a new car. At the same time he was aware that the surrounding air was filled with a lingering smell of the burned house.

"She's been kidnapped!" exclaimed Jane Kline, staring at the empty car, her lips trembling. "Something has happened to her."

Dick took his wife in his arms and tried to comfort her. Best to keep moving, he thought. They toured the Moyer property. Dick didn't want to dwell on the thought, but was it possible that his daughter, dazed from an accident, had stumbled into the ruins? They approached the charred timbers and peered intently into the wreckage of the newly built home. Neither spoke.

The cellar, cast in ominous shadows in the fading light, was nearly filled with brackish water and debris. Dick looked for a white uniform, but everything in the cellar was black, burned. Debbie was not there.

Chief Gingrich was in his cruiser, radioing for more information. When the Klines returned, they told him they would continue on the road home and search for their daughter.

"She's been taken from us," said Jane softly. They backed out of the driveway and continued slowly down the road, pausing now and again to look on the shoulder, and beyond that into the fields, now barely visible in the dusk.

A few moments after the Klines left, another car pulled up behind the policeman's. It was Debbie's brother Frank. He had stopped by the house and discovered from a neighbor that his sister was missing. When he saw her abandoned car, he suspected the worst.

"I'll kill the bastard when I get my hands on him!" he exclaimed to the police chief, clenching his fists.

Within the hour a small search party was formed. Dick and Jane Kline, with Frank, their eldest son, led separate groups into the surrounding areas and back roads.

About the same time, a fireman who had volunteered to keep an eye on the abandoned car noticed handprints on the trunk. He hoped the slight drizzle wouldn't erase the imprints in the dust.

Trooper Paul Ciprich hoped it would be a quiet Friday evening. It seemed sleepy enough. Perhaps the comforting blanket of the warm summer night would prevent the usual family squabbles that always seemed to erupt shortly after payday.

Ciprich pushed a lock of dark hair from his forehead. He had a boyish face and a quick smile, but the smile was sometimes deceiving. He took his job seriously. Aside from his family, it was the focal point of his life. He had been a criminal investigator for ten years and a state trooper for most of his adult life, both at the Chambersburg barracks. He loved the area, with its rolling hills and wooded mountainsides, and he enjoyed hiking into the wilderness, a paperback in his pocket and a fishing rod over his shoulder. If the trout weren't biting, he could escape into the book. But the hikes were, in the end, a diversion, for he was always anxious to return to the barracks, where he thrived on the investigative work. As always, though, he hoped there would be nothing to investigate, that Franklin County would continue to drowse in the heat.

But, in the still air, it seemed that something was about to happen. Ciprich had developed a sixth sense after years of experience, and he waited, drumming his fingers on the desk. When the call came in, he was almost relieved.

A girl was missing, her car had been found, abandoned, and Ciprich had requested assistance in processing it. "Missing Persons," in his experience, did not usually remain missing for long. Especially the young ones. Most left home for only a short time and then returned to outraged parents. And most were genuinely sorry for the concern they caused their families. Others would leave home again and again, seeking attention.

But there were those few, he well knew, who never made it home again.

"This must have been one hell of a fire," said Ciprich to the local policeman who met him at the Moyer property. He stood with his hands in his pockets, surveying the wreckage.

"You could see the red reflection in the sky for miles around," said the man. "When I first saw the red glow, I thought it was the country club going up. The fire chief suspects arson, and we're conducting an investigation. The place was brand new. The folks who built it hadn't even moved in yet. Good thing, I guess."

Ciprich peered down into the cellar as the policeman described the abandoned car, the missing girl, and her worried parents. He had three daughters of his own, and he immediately felt a sympathetic camaraderie for the Klines.

"The Klines think she was nabbed," said the policeman. "And from what I know of her, she wasn't the runaway type."

Ciprich nodded. He continued to look thoughtfully at the cellar.

"Anybody check in there?" he asked softly.

"We checked it out. But it wasn't a thorough search. It was too damned dark, and the parents were here. I didn't really *want* to find anything, if you know what I mean."

"I understand," said Ciprich. He had investigated more than a dozen local murders, and unexpected discoveries never failed to shock even the most seasoned troopers. "See if you can round up some volunteers. We'll make a full-scale search of this place and the surrounding area tomorrow. Right now I'd like to take a look at that car."

In Shockey's Garage the burgundy Vega looked small, almost forlorn. One of the policemen from the Waynesboro station met Ciprich there. He seemed apologetic.

"A hundred people must have pawed this thing before I got to it," he said, gesturing helplessly at the trunk. "And the rain didn't help. I thought we ought to call in the experts."

Ciprich examined the telltale marks where the prints had been lifted and agreed. "I'll get someone down from Harrisburg. This job needs a light touch."

And he reflected ruefully that the policeman's estimation of the number of hands that had contaminated the car was conservative. As he left the garage, he hiked up his pants and brushed back his hair, and steeled himself for an interview with the Klines.

"She's been taken from us," her mother said again, weeping. Her husband looked helplessly on. He was a powerfully built man, and Ciprich pitied any kidnapper he got his hands on. But now his great strength was of little help.

"She's been taken," repeated Mrs. Kline. "Taken and killed."

It was obvious that neither had slept, and Ciprich could imagine their sense of frustration as he tried to assure them that everything that *could* be done *would* be done. Dick Kline vowed to join the search party and made it clear he could not be dissuaded. Ciprich had to admire him for that.

An hour later, as Ciprich pulled out of the Klines' driveway and headed toward Waynesboro Hospital, he experienced a curious sinking sensation. Dick and Jane Kline had presented a picture of a beautiful girl who was dutiful in her studies, interested in church and civic duties, and thoroughly responsible. Not the type to run away, and certainly not the type to leave her new car behind if she *had* decided to take off for a few days.

The employees at the hospital confirmed the Kline's estimation of Debbie.

"Run away?" asked one of the women who worked with her in the cafeteria. "Not on your life. Not Debbie. She was going straight home to take her mom and dad out to dinner. No, she's not the runaway kind."

Ciprich was beginning to believe it. As he left the hospital, daylight was fading, and with it his hopes of finding, unharmed, the pretty young girl who had vanished just twenty-four hours before.

THREE

Saturday, July 24

Bob Cox, assistant managing editor of Waynesboro's *Record Herald*, was putting the Saturday paper to bed. He could hear the low hum of the air conditioners and knew that outside the temperature was already beginning to rise. It was a pleasant way to spend a Saturday morning, laying out the news, making it fit into a cohesive picture of the world.

When the telephone rang, he automatically looked at the clock. It was 9:45 A.M.

"Bob, this is Paul Ciprich."

Cox recognized the voice. He had worked with the trooper on other occasions and admired his no-nonsense approach to investigative work.

"I'm calling from the Shockey Garage. We have a fingerprint expert here from the Harrisburg crime lab. We're dusting the missing girl's car, and I'd like you to get a picture of it. Can you send a photographer down? We're organizing a search party, and I think we're going to need all the publicity we can get on this."

Cox readily assented. Ciprich was not the headline-hunting type, and if he wanted publicity, it must be important to the investigation. Cox had run a story on Debbie Kline in Friday's paper. He had children of his own, and he hoped, staring at her snapshot, that she would turn up as a runaway. A young girl off on a spree.

As he went about his business, checking the final copy and glancing at the wire services, he mused on the trooper's call. Had he said *manhunt* or *body search?*

Steven J. Davidock, the fingerprint expert from the Harrisburg crime lab, was discouraged. The Vega was so covered with dust that it was impossible to lift prints off the exterior.

"I can't do a thing with this," he said to Paul Ciprich. "Let's try the inside."

A mechanic, wiping his greasy hands on a rag, watched the two officers.

"Hell, everybody and his brother had his hands on that thing," he said, gesturing around the garage.

Ciprich and the mechanic, Richard Lingenfelter, looked at each other. That much was obvious to both of them. Ciprich pushed the front seat forward, leaned into the back with a vacuum cleaner, and proceeded to collect every particle of hair and dust. It was probably a futile effort, he thought, but sometimes a case was built on the most minute piece of evidence.

He found Debbie's wallet in the glove compartment.

"Damn it," he moaned, showing it to Lingenfelter. It contained the usual cards and photos. And thirty-eight dollars in cash.

That cinched it. Debbie Kline wasn't a runaway. No one running away from home would leave cash behind.

With a sense of grim interest he and Lingenfelter took the car apart. They found nothing, not even a single print worthy of microscopic examination. The Vega was a dead end.

Lingenfelter and Davidock drove the car back to the Kline residence. Ciprich followed in the police cruiser. The entire family was gathered in the front yard when he pulled into the driveway.

Jane Kline, crying, ran inside the house as Lingenfelter unwound his lanky form from behind the wheel. Dick Kline stood with his arms folded, a silent, melancholy giant. His other children looked sadly at Debbie's car. Lingenfelter went inside to talk with Jane Kline, while Ciprich showed Dick the wallet.

Dick confirmed that it was his daughter's.

"It looks bad, doesn't it?" he said.

Ciprich tried to be noncommital. Inside the house, Jane Kline, informed of the wallet's recovery, broke down completely. Lingenfelter questioned her as delicately as he could, given the circumstances. But there were things he had to ask. Jane flared up when he touched on subjects that even remotely called her daughter's reputation into question.

"Deborah Sue is a good girl. She didn't even have a steady boyfriend. She's been kidnapped. Or worse," she sobbed. Lingenfelter was powerless to help her.

"We'll do what we can, ma'am," he said gently.

It was brutally hot at the Moyer place. About fifty volunteers were gathered around a cruiser, waiting. Sweat poured down their faces. It was ninety degrees and would get hotter as the day progressed. On the trunk of the cruiser a state trooper had spread out a large map of the area. He drew a circle, then cut it into grids for assignment. Most of the volunteers were armed with long sticks. They would be wading through deep, snake-infested brush.

Ken Peiffer, the *Record Herald* photographer, was snapping pictures of the burned-out cellar. The debris had been gone over with a rake, then sifted, but nothing of consequence had been found. Bob Cox left the group of volunteers and joined him.

"Something stinks," he said, jerking his thumb at the ruins. "And I don't mean this damned rubble. Paul Ciprich found her wallet right in the car. It looks like an abduction."

Both men joined in the search. Peiffer, who was afraid of snakes, stuck resolutely to the main roads, while Cox waded deep into the underbrush. The palm of heat tightened into a fist as the volunteers fanned out into the countryside. All were silently hoping there would be no grisly discoveries, and as the day wore on, this hope remained.

But Deborah Sue Kline was still missing.

Later that day, Cox and Peiffer interviewed her father, whose unyielding determination had inspired the search party.

"I don't believe she left of her own free will," he said. "She had everything going for her."

Dick Kline pounded a fist into his open hand as, in frustration, he listed the reasons why he felt his daughter had not run off. She had a good job and had just bought a new car. She would never have left the car with the windows down, and she would not have left her makeup and wallet in the glove compartment and the keys in the ignition.

"Debbie was abducted, and we've got to find her," he said emphatically, near tears. He walked away, head bowed, to compose himself.

"I suspect somebody grabbed her and has taken her someplace," Trooper Lingenfelter confided to the two reporters. "I'm hoping we'll get a call in a day or two from somebody, saying they're holding her someplace—or word that the girl has been found wandering along the road, or something to that effect. That's what I hope."

Peiffer suddenly had a thought. He wondered if this case had any connection to a murder he'd covered in the summer of 1972.

"Is this kid any relation to Leroy Kline?" he asked. Peiffer had been there when Leroy's body had been found, less than two miles from where he was now standing. An autopsy revealed that he had been stomped to death. Three men had been arrested and convicted of manslaughter.

"Yes," was the answer. "He was her uncle."

They fell silent as Dick Kline returned, carrying a large book under his arm. He opened it to an inside page and showed the two reporters a picture of his daughter.

"Read the caption underneath," he suggested.

She likes music, animals, drawing, taking walks, the caption read.

"You'll have to excuse me now," said Kline. "The doctor has put my wife under sedation to calm her. I'll have to go home."

He walked away, his strong back rippling under his short-sleeved shirt. The yearbook was clutched in his hand. The two reporters looked at each other, then walked to their car.

The ride home was silent.

FOUR

The First Week

Paul Ciprich organized a full-scale investigation. The runaway theory had been discounted, and no one had contacted the Klines for ransom. His instincts told him it had probably been an abduction, possibly a rape, and—although he didn't want to worry the Kline's without just cause—the possibility of murder was not remote. And yet the investigation and the additional searches were conceived with the assumption that Deborah Sue Kline was still alive.

"We mustn't get discouraged," he told Corporal John Farrell. "Not yet."

The fire department continued its probe of the mysterious fire that had leveled the Moyer home. The Vega had been hidden there, that much now seemed obvious, and some connection between the two cases was possible. They conjectured that Debbie might have witnessed the fire, been seen by the arsonists, and then abducted to ensure her silence.

An investigator drove to the Klines' house on Sunday. Dick and Jane greeted him with smiles, hoping he had brought positive news.

Their hope died when he asked about her whereabouts on the night of the fire.

"She was home before midnight," Dick told him. "We woke her up when we heard the sirens and saw the glow in the sky."

Meanwhile, Lingenfelter and Farrell were questioning known sex offenders, especially those in the southern part of the county. John Farrell checked his voluminous files. Most were dormant—men who had been caught once, sentenced, and never charged again. Others were "repeaters," arrested again and again for similar crimes. Farrell questioned them all. However, each alibi checked out.

When Mrs. Kline told Lingenfelter that her daughter was religious, he decided to pursue that angle. A religious cult had recently come into the area, and a local policeman told him that an elderly man had been talked into putting his life savings in the hands of the group, with a guarantee that he would receive a lucrative return on his investment. This seemed suspicious to Lingenfelter, and the cult, warned that he was about to investigate, left the area the same day.

After determining that Debbie was not with the group, he talked with one of her friends, who scoffed at the idea.

"Sure, Debbie was religious. She read the Bible. She went to church. But she wasn't interested in any crazy cults. She thought that sort of thing was sacrilegious."

Another dead end. But they were obliged to follow up all possible leads, no matter how improbable. It was impossible to know just where a productive lead might turn up.

While Lingenfelter had been following up the cult, Farrell had been checking on the Leroy Kline case. Debbie's uncle had been murdered, stomped to death by a group of men. Now his niece was missing. Farrell discovered that both Dick Kline and his son Frank had testified at the trial that they had heard an old truck driving past the Kline residence on the night of the murder. While their testimony was not damaging, it established a time for the police investigators.

Debbie had not been involved in the investigation in any way, Farrell noted, but one of the three men convicted in the crime had made threatening remarks against her family while he was a prisoner. And all three had since been released from jail.

One of the men was working locally in the farm-implement business. Another was in construction. The third was studying to become a minister.

And all three had perfect alibis.

On Monday Paul Ciprich joined Lingenfelter at the home of Sarah Atkins, who lived not far from the Moyer property.

"I think you better hear this," Lingenfelter told him.

"Right after supper, maybe about six o'clock or thereabouts, I was sitting on my front porch. A yellow Volkswagen went by. There were two men in it. One of them had black hair; the other was blond. The car was making such a racket I guess something must have been wrong with the engine. They weren't going very fast, but they looked kind of hurried, if you know what I mean. The car was bright yellow. I know it was a Volkswagen because my brother had one just like it," Sarah told him.

There was little traffic in the area, and a car in the general vicinity at the right time was clue enough for Ciprich. A description of the car was circulated immediately. New- and used-car dealers were contacted. Auto paint shops were asked if they had recently painted a VW bright yellow.

The search was redoubled when a local couple reported having seen two men in the vicinity of the Moyer property shortly after six o'clock on the evening Debbie disappeared. Two cars had been parked in the dirt driveway, they said. A young man with reddish, sandy hair and a beard stood next to one car. He was wearing a short-sleeved shirt. Behind him another man with dark hair, wearing a uniform shirt, crouched behind the second car.

Two different sources had placed someone near the Moyer property at the time of the disappearance.

Then a third source came forth. Sam Mowen reported seeing a young man walking along the shoulder of Gehr Road, not far from the Moyer property, at about 6:45 P.M. The young man had caught his attention as he was driving home from his construction job.

"He stared at my car when I slowed down, but he never stopped walking. I thought it was kind of odd," he said.

The man had bushy black hair, a mustache, and piercing eyes. Sam remembered the eyes especially, and he agreed to help one of the troopers put together a composite photograph.

While Mowen selected various facial traits from the composite-likeness kit to create a portrait of the possible suspect, Ciprich went to Lancaster to follow up a curious report.

A truck driver recalled seeing a car pass him, going in the other direction, not far from the Moyer property. He noticed a girl waving to him from the back seat of the blue car. Two or three men were in the front, but he couldn't be sure. At the time he'd been more curious than alarmed, but he did think enough of the incident to take down the license number.

There was one snag. When he heard about the Kline girl's disappearance and looked for the scrap of paper, he realized that he had discarded the scrap with his old newspapers, which had been picked up by the local Wayside Mission the day before in its weekly paper collection.

Paul Ciprich and another officer from the Lancaster barracks spent the next two days sifting through more than a ton of paper at the mission.

They found nothing.

Later that week Farrell and Dick Kline returned to the Moyer property. Kline was a man obsessed. He had to find Debbie alive, and find her he must. His wife was still under sedation, and he was concerned about her health.

Kline had some of his daughter's clothing with him, and he presented it to the state police K-9 search team. The bloodhound "Vellie," a big, friendly dog, was primed with the scent and they started on a cross-country trek. Four men followed the animal on a meandering trail, but each time they returned to the spot where the burgundy Vega had been abandoned. They continued the search for hours, hoping to cross Debbie's trail.

But finally the bloodhound stopped and looked up at them with sad eyes, panting. There was no trail, no scent to follow. Dick Kline returned home to look after his wife.

The *Record Herald* kept the story on page one, hoping the publicity would generate some helpful leads. And shortly after the composite photo was run, several phone calls were logged.

Checking out information received from one of the calls, a local investigator, armed with a copy of the composite picture, was startled to find himself face to face with a man who was a dead ringer for the face in the picture. He worked for an area garbage-disposal business.

"Do you know Debbie Kline?" he was asked.

"No."

"Did you walk on the Gehr Road last Thursday anywhere near the Moyer property?"

He shook his head, staring at his interrogator with the same piercing eyes Sam Mowen had described.

"I don't see a car here. How do you get around?"

"Walk."

"Do you ever walk the Gehr Road?"

He hesitated. "Yes."

"Did you walk the Gehr Road last Thursday?"

"No!"

An hour later the investigator returned. He had talked to another person, who said he had given the man a ride to Gehr Road on the night in question. He shrugged this off but agreed to take a lie-detector test.

The trooper who administered the test shook his head. "I don't think this guy is too well glued together. But I think he knows right from wrong and yes from no, so the polygraph should give us a good indication if he's lying."

They interrogated him for more than two hours, returning again and again to the evening of July 22, to the vicinity of Gehr Road, to the disappearance of eighteen-year-old Deborah Sue Kline. But the needle did not budge. He was not lying.

Another search was organized for Saturday, July 30. Members of the Pennsylvania National Guard volunteered. The Franklin County Civil Defense System, the Citizen's-Band Organization, the Mountain Valley Saddle Club, and numerous private citizens offered to assist.

More than a hundred men and women converged on the Moyer property. Methodically, they combed a three-mile search area.

Richard Lingenfelter, accompanying the National Guard in

a jeep, discovered a pair of women's pink bikini panties off a back road in a spot that was obviously a lovers park. They were shown to Mrs. Kline, who positively said they did not belong to Debbie.

Nine days had passed. The investigators had checked out the yellow Volkswagen and the blue car. They had questioned the mustached man. They had talked with friends and relatives. They had conducted two major searches. And not a clue had been found.

The trail was growing cold.

FIVE

The Second Week

Ken Peiffer was organizing what promised to be a routine day when the operator signaled a call for him. He picked up the phone absent-mindedly.

"Young man, who are you?" asked the shaky voice of an elderly woman.

Peiffer identified himself and asked who was calling. Either his question went unheard or he was being politely ignored.

"I asked the operator to connect me with someone who was involved in the stories about the missing girl," the woman continued. "If it ain't you, then connect me with the right person, and you'll have to speak up, 'cause I can't hear too good."

Peiffer glanced up. The operator was pointing frantically to her ears to indicate that the caller was hard of hearing.

He yelled into the phone. "My name is Kenneth Peiffer, and I know about the Debbie Kline case!"

Everyone in the office looked up. The AP teletype machine chose that moment to stop its clattering transmission. In the sudden echoing silence Peiffer felt his face go red.

"Don't shout, dearie. I ain't deaf," said the old woman. "If you're the right one, then I have something to tell you."

"Go ahead," said Peiffer in his normal voice. He tried to ignore the half-dozen people observing him with amusement.

"Speak up," she demanded. "I told you we had a bad connection."

"I said I'm listening!" shouted Peiffer. Several reporters filed in, grinning, and Peiffer knew his cheeks were flaming.

"That's better, dearie. My name is Mazie Rank. And the missing girl is living here with me."

"What!" This time Peiffer's voice really rocked the office, and his grinning audience dissolved into laughter.

"It would suit me better if you didn't scream into the telephone, young man. I said the young girl is living in my house, in a room upstairs."

"Are you sure?" he inquired. If this was a crank call, it wouldn't be the first they had received on the Kline case.

A trace of righteous indignation could be detected in the woman's reply. "She's living upstairs, I tell you. I rented the room to her. She's a very nice girl, you know."

Peiffer took down the woman's name and address and promised to go right over. What if Debbie *had* wandered off, in a state of amnesia, say. Wasn't it possible that some old woman might take her in? He called police headquarters.

An hour later officers Lingenfelter and Farrell joined Peiffer. The old woman's house was located on one of the steepest streets in the city, and after trudging up the walkway and a long flight of steps, all three men were out of breath. Mazie Rank opened her door a crack and surveyed them skeptically. She was a tiny, bird-like woman, thin and wrinkled with age, but her eyes were bright and shining.

"You the deaf fellow from the *Record Herald*?"

Lingenfelter and Farrell eyed the reporter, who found himself blushing again. Mazie ushered them inside. She seemed happy to have company as she led them up a flight of stairs to the room where her "missing girl" was living.

"She ain't here right now. That's why I called." She indicated a small bedroom. "And right here is where she sleeps."

"Do you mind if we look around?" asked Corporal Farrell.

"Help yourself, young man," she said happily. "I'll be right downstairs when you're done. Maybe she'll be back by then."

It was obvious the room was being occupied by a young person. The magazines found on the nightstand were those that might appeal to a young woman.

It was Lingenfelter who discovered the papers.

"Damn! Look at this," he exclaimed, holding out a sheaf of yellow, legal-size papers. The sheets contained written notes describing the human body, specifically dealing with the breakdown of the anatomy. They could have been the notes of someone studying to be a nurse. And Debbie Kline had been working at Waynesboro Hospital.

But their excitement was dampened when Farrell discovered a number of half-filled pill bottles in the medicine cabinet containing prescriptions from a New Jersey pharmacy and bearing the address of a New Jersey woman.

Mazie Rank reluctantly identified the notes as belonging to her niece, who had stayed there sometime ago. Although uneasy about the discovery, she agreed that Lingenfelter could keep the notes "while he studied it."

"But after my niece left, the Kline girl came here to live," she tried to assure them. "I recognized her the minute I saw her picture in the paper. You believe me, don't you?"

When she saw the doubt on their faces, she began to plead

with them. "Just because she ain't here now doesn't mean she wasn't here at all, does it?"

It was obvious to the investigators that she was a lonely old woman. Neighbors informed them that she often imagined things, and that no one had lived with her since her niece had returned to New Jersey. Lingenfelter filed the anatomy notes.

Like Mazie Rank, he, too, wished Debbie had been living there.

Cox took the next call. The woman, sobbing and hysterical, had been trying to reach the police, but the exchange was busy. Instead, she called the *Record Herald*. In a small city, the daily newspaper often served as a focus for the disturbed and the distraught, and Cox had handled many such calls.

"He said he'd kill me. He said he'd cut me up like the Kline girl. He said all kinds of filthy things," the woman sobbed.

Slowly, as he tried to calm her, he pieced the story together. A man had called. He had a slight southern accent and sounded as though he were young, perhaps in his late twenties.

"You answer all my questions," he had said to the terrified woman, "or I'll kill you just like I did Debbie."

The woman said she was too frightened to hang up immediately, so she continued to listen to the hypnotic, insistent voice. The voice informed her that he knew what time she left work, what kind of car she drove, and that he had been watching her. He wanted to rape her; he was *going* to rape her. It might not happen that week, or that month, or even that year. He would be waiting until she let down her guard, and when she least expected it, he would leap and strike.

The mysterious caller knew she worked at the hospital—the same hospital where Debbie worked—and he knew what shift she had. He knew that her husband was away. He repeated his threats, describing in lewd detail exactly how he would rape her, and how he would then cut her up.

After Cox had transferred her call to the police, he put down the phone and sighed. Similar calls had been reported all week. A man, or perhaps more than one, had terrified a number of the women who worked at Waynesboro Hospital. And to make matters more insidious, the caller usually knew the first name of the woman—most of whom were married, and most of whom had their numbers listed in their husbands' names.

Somebody had done a little research. They might be only crank calls: The mysterious disappearance of a young girl from a small town always seemed to bring the nuts out of the woodwork, but they were exceptionally chilling calls, implying, as they did, that Deborah Sue Kline had been murdered.

The rash of calls also disturbed Paul Ciprich. A blanket of fear was being spread over the town. Frightened people often hesitated before cooperating with the police, and such terror could adversely affect his investigation of the Kline disappearance.

And now it was more than crank calls.

Several of the women who worked at Waynesboro Hospital reported that they had been followed home from work. One had nearly lost control of her car when another vehicle slammed into her rear bumper, as though to force her off the road. It was difficult to attribute that sort of behavior to a mere crank, someone who had been stirred up by the publicity the case had generated.

When he heard that one woman had received her second obscene call, Ciprich swung into action. The woman had had the presence of mind to know she might help trap the caller if she appeared to cooperate with him. She agreed to meet him the following evening in the hospital parking lot.

Ciprich and three plainclothesmen staked out the parking lot.

They had hidden themselves hours before, in hopes the man would not be frightened off.

At dusk a car pulled into the lot. Ciprich tensed, pulling himself out of a daydream. The woman waited a few moments and then climbed languidly out of her car. She arranged her hair, studying her face in a compact mirror, then lit up a cigarette. They waited.

They waited for two hours. No one showed.

Peiffer reported a lead he had received from Debbie's sister. She and a friend were sharing hamburgers and cokes at a fast-food restaurant. Their conversation was disrupted when suddenly they became aware that someone was taking their picture. Two men were smiling at them. One held a camera. Debbie's sister was disturbed. The young men were dressed outlandishly, and something about their expressions made her cringe. They snapped a few more pictures and left when the girls continued to ignore them.

Debbie's sister thought they might have belonged to the religious cult that had recently been soliciting in the area. Peiffer referred the information to the state police. The cult had wandered through several towns in Pennsylvania; members came and went. None had criminal records. None was sexually disturbed in any obvious way. None fit the description Sam Mowen had given.

The incident remained a mystery.

The disappearance affected different people in different ways. The husbands of the harassed women who worked at Waynesboro Hospital began to take time off from their jobs to drive their wives to and from work. Police escorts were given whenever requested, especially for the night shift. The townspeople began to stay in after dark, submitting to a self-imposed curfew.

Strangers in town were greeted brusquely, if at all. Parents watched the clock when their children were due home, and more than one hysterical mother had raced to the school only to find her children perfectly safe, having been kept after for extra work or having gone home with a classmate.

In Waynesboro the shadows had become ominous.

Wednesday night, August 11, twenty-one days after Deborah Sue Kline disappeared, screams were heard in the vicinity of the Old Forge area at Chimney Rocks, a part of the Appalachian Trail. A number of people heard the blood-curdling screams and said they had come from a girl.

People speculated that Debbie was alive, held captive at Chimney Rocks. The police organized another search team. But Thursday morning's search was fruitless. No one was found, and, moreover, it appeared no one had been in the area recently.

But at noon a pair of white shoes was found near the cinder pile along Route 16. Debbie had been wearing white shoes as part of her hospital uniform. And later that afternoon a white uniform was found near the intersection of Country Club and Gehr roads. Both items were turned over to the authorities, who began a methodical examination to determine if they were, indeed, Debbie's.

The soles of the shoes were heavily worn, too heavily for the three weeks Debbie had been employed at the hospital. And Mrs. Kline positively identified the uniform as not belonging to her daughter. Debbie had been wearing a white pantsuit. The uniform found on Gehr Road was a dress suit.

Jane Kline was still on medication. She had lost thirty-five pounds.

If Debbie had in fact been abducted, the abductors were still at large, and the police made a special effort to warn teenage girls to ignore the solicitations of older men and especially to shun rides from strangers.

At 7:15 one August night, Ronald Henninger, his wife, and his attractive stepdaughter, Candy Jo, arrived at the Greencastle police headquarters to swear out a complaint.

Candy Jo was fourteen but looked older. She was exceptionally pretty, with long dark hair that fell below her shoulders. And there was every indication that she had narrowly escaped a dangerous situation.

She explained what had happened to the police.

"I met a man who lives right out of town around here. He asked me if I wanted to go for a ride in his car and I said OK. It was a beautiful day. He had some beer with him, and I got thirsty and decided to drink some. It was real hot in the car. I guess I must have gotten drunk. After a while I don't remember much of anything."

She glanced at her stepfather, who was understandably agitated.

"Do you know what time you went for the ride?" she was asked.

"It must have been about one o'clock."

"What happened then? What time did he bring you home?"

"I think around five o'clock," she said dully, glancing again at her stepfather.

"Did anything happen? Did he make any advances or threaten you in any way?"

Before answering, she looked at her parents, then at the floor between her knees. She had pulled her feet back under the chair.

"Not that I remember," she said, avoiding the policeman's eyes. "I guess I was sort of out of it."

She paused, then blurted out, "He ran me through a car wash!"

"Well, I'll be damned," said the policeman. Looking at the defiant young girl, he couldn't help but grin.

"When I got home from work," interjected her stepfather, "there she was, sprawled across her bed, soaking wet. That man should be locked up!"

The policeman turned to the girl. "Will you sign a statement to that effect?"

Some moments elapsed before the embarrassed girl could reply. She seemed to be seeking a cue from her mother. Finally, in a barely audible voice, she answered in the affirmative.

"We have to be sure of this now. Sure you are not mistaken. If you made a mistake, your charge might ruin this man for the rest of his life," the policeman warned.

The girl assured him she spoke the truth, and a warrant was issued for the arrest of the man who had run Candy Jo Henninger through a car wash.

"You had better straighten up and stop taking rides," the policeman warned the girl. "I understand you're very young, but you just can't do things like that. Not in this day and age. Do you want to be like that Kline girl and show up missing some day?"

Her stepfather turned white and wheeled around on his heels. He looked as though he was about to be sick.

"Sorry," the cop apologized.

As the family left the station, he reflected that people had become extremely sensitive to the Kline case.

On August 19, Jane Kline's plea for information appeared in the *Record Herald*.

"I just wish anyone who may have any information, no matter how trivial it may seem, would either contact us or the police. I know Debbie didn't run away. I just hope someone has a soft spot in his heart and will come forward and tell us what they know or what they might suspect. No names need be signed. I just can't go on like this. Not knowing is the worst part."

The Klines had resigned themselves to the fact that Debbie was abducted against her will. Possibly she had been raped—or worse. But they continued their vigil, hoping she would be returned, or return of her own accord.

Jane Kline confided her fears to Cox.

"I know Debbie was afraid of the dark. One night she and I walked up the road. She heard something in the bushes and started to run. When I didn't run fast enough, she took me by the hand and started pulling. I nearly broke my wrist when she ran around one side of a tree and me the other. She was afraid of the dark."

SIX

Dead Ends

Trooper Paul Ciprich sighed. He felt as though the Kline case had backed him against an impregnable wall. The barracks' telephones had logged hundreds of calls, all of which had been followed up, yet not one substantial lead had developed.

Ciprich sat back in his swivel chair, his hands behind his head, and stared off into space. His fellow troopers knew better than to disturb him when he assumed that pose. He believed it was probable that a killer was on the loose. Somehow, somewhere, something had to be done about it. He couldn't consider Franklin County safe until the case had been solved—one way or the other. And certainly the Klines would never be able to rest until their daughter's disappearance had been explained.

Ciprich rolled up his shirt sleeves and began to sift through the evidence, hoping to discern a pattern.

Strange reports had been received from the Chimney Rocks location. Screams continued to be heard in the early morning hours. Investigators continued to search in that region, which by now had been trampled by numerous curiosity seekers, making any discovery of hard evidence less likely.

Particles of flesh and something that might have been bone were unearthed. These were taken to police labs and analyzed. Two days later the final verdict came back.

Not human.

Volunteers still clamored to help. One Sunday afternoon the Chambersburg Friendship Fire Company's underwater rescue team of scuba divers searched a water-filled quarry at Williamson. It was an eerie location. The search was directed from a small til boat, and shouts echoed from the quarry walls. The divers systematically explored the murky waters, returning again and again to the central boat until the chilly water began to tax their endurance.

They found lost objects, bed springs, and other refuse—but no bodies.

State park attendants continued to make special efforts to comb remote areas open to the public on a year-round basis. Foresters spent untold hours traveling through the dense woods surrounding the valley. They attempted to pinpoint the locations over which buzzards circled in the hot August sky.

Wherever signs of fresh digging were located, the earth was turned over and probed. Many dead animals were unearthed, but no human corpses.

And there were those whose sick minds were stimulated by the same publicity that had spurred others to offer assistance.

The Klines, whose telephone number at the time was unlisted, received a number of anonymous calls. On consecutive days two mysterious messages were received, contributing to Jane Kline's ill health. She had answered the first call, but the caller hung up after a short pause.

Dick, seeking to protect his wife's nerves, answered the phone the next day.

"I picked up the phone and said, 'hello, hello.' I kept saying 'hello,' but no one answered me. I guess it must have been a full minute before the person hung up."

Dick had heard background noises similar to traffic, and he thought the call might have come from a public telephone booth. He had in mind the booth in the hospital parking lot, where Debbie kept her car. And he was still hoping for a ransom call from whoever had kidnapped his daughter.

Now more than ever he was convinced she had been abducted. Anyone wanting ransom money would try to keep her alive—or so he hoped.

Cox ran another description of Debbie Kline, and in it he mentioned that she was last seen wearing a gold Timex watch with an expansion bracelet. She also might, according to her mother, have been wearing a gold chain necklace with a star pendant.

He also ran a letter from Jane Kline. One night, unable to sleep, she had written:

> Today my heart is so full of hurt and sorrow and tears that I can hardly stand it. My family has been affected by this horrible thing that has happened to our lives and to our daughter Debbie. So again I write and ask someone, anyone, for any help

they can give us. If tears and prayer could bring Debbie back home, we would have had her back long ago. . . . Please, I am pouring out my heart to you for help. I will do anything you ask. Please return Debbie to us. If your information leads us to Debbie, the reward you ask will be paid.

Dick Kline had walked the newsmen to their car when they left with his wife's heartrending letter. Jane Kline was helpless, willing to grasp at straws, and writing was some comfort to her. Their car was parked behind Debbie's Vega, which sparkled in the late summer sun.

"We're still making the payments for her," said Kline. He paused. "We'll keep up the payments until she comes home, if ever . . ."

He couldn't finish. After a long minute of uncomfortable silence, he added, "I think she is dead."

Dick Kline turned and walked back into the house, head bowed low.

A few days after the description of Debbie's watch and necklace appeared in the *Record Herald,* her cousin received a package in the mail. No return address was given. The young girl was not expecting a gift, but she opened the box with unrestrained excitement.

Inside was a gold-colored necklace with a star pendant. No note was attached. Jane Kline examined the necklace and said that although it was of a similar type, it was not her daughter's.

It was never determined who sent the necklace, or why.

Mrs. Donald Yeager wanted to do something for the Klines. Her heart went out to them, for she could imagine how she would feel if one of her own children were missing, and with everyone in town assuming the worst. Mrs. Yeager believed in God, in a wise, loving God—and she believed implicitly in the power of prayer.

She decided to hold a prayer service for Debbie. She felt that the joined power of group prayer might help Debbie, and certainly the effort would be appreciated by her parents. They would know that the community was with them, in heart and in deed.

The night after the prayer service was announced in the *Record Herald,* Mrs. Yeager called Bob Cox. Hearing a thump on the front porch, she had gone to investigate. Two pieces of raw liver had been thrown there, still moist with blood. One was wrapped in regular butcher's paper. The other was twisted into the shape of a rope.

Why on earth would anyone do such a thing? she wanted to know. Was it a teenage prank, or did the raw meat have some possible significance?

Cox didn't know.

In an apparently unrelated matter, the investigation into the July fire that leveled the new home of Reverend Moyer five days before Debbie disappeared was concluded. The blaze was described as incendiary in origin. If indeed it had been arson, the arsonist was still at large.

At Peiffer's suggestion, a new telephone was installed at the Kline residence, with its number publicly listed. The action, noted in the *Record Herald,* brought a flood of calls. Most were from well wishers and sympathizers. But many were crank calls. Dick Kline got so that he hated to hear it ring, although he always hurried to answer it. He and Jane were still hoping to hear from the kidnappers.

One teenage girl made three separate calls to the Klines, requesting information about the handprints on the trunk of Debbie's Vega. Police stepped in when it became obvious that she was just harassing the bereaved parents.

It was now common knowledge that an unspecified reward was being offered for any information that would lead to Debbie's discovery, and this may have prompted some of the calls.

However, the Klines were not the only ones being harassed. The list of women who had received threatening calls began to resemble the local telephone directory. Nearly every woman who worked at the hospital, from nurses to kitchen employees, had received at least one call. Oddly enough, most of the calls were received when the women were alone. It was as though they were being watched.

Some were followed home, regardless of the time of day.

One woman in the hospital housekeeping department told police she was resigning at the end of the week.

"My life is worth far more than the salary I receive," she stated flatly. She told police she suspected another hospital employee was about to be snatched.

In a baffling case with no solid leads, no concrete evidence, everyone came under suspicion.

Police were notified when a woman was treated at Waynesboro Hospital for cuts and bruises. She had been beaten by the male companion she lived with. A routine check on his background revealed that he had a history of such abuse, and his first wife had left him for that reason. A closer check revealed that he was obsessed with guns and firearms. As an added point of interest to the investigators, he had been discharged from a fire company in another state when it was suspected, but never proven, that he was responsible for a number of blazes.

Could he have been responsible for the Moyer fire? The car he drove matched the description of one seen in the area at roughly the time Debbie's car was abandoned. He was the object of scrutiny for several days and was finally questioned by investigators.

He had an ironclad alibi.

An elementary-school teacher was driving home from work one particularly warm afternoon, when her car was blocked by another on Old Forge Road. She managed to pass the vehicle and speed away—or so she thought. Looking in the rearview mirror, she was terrified to discover that the car was now close behind her. Trying to control her growing panic, she hit the accelerator. The car stayed with her, as though glued to her bumper. She could clearly see the driver. He had long black hair, dark eyes, a large nose, and was clean shaven. His expression was threatening, and she speeded up to 80 mph before she managed to shake him on the long, winding road.

The four-door, cream-colored car had Maryland tags, and the woman had been able to catch the first three digits. Maryland officials were contacted. But three digits weren't enough, and they drew another blank.

The school teacher was especially shaken. Debbie Kline was a friend of hers.

The police, for all their effort, seemed to be getting nowhere.

Three men, affluent friends of the Kline family, hired a private investigator from Maryland to assist in the search. They hoped that someone working undercover might be able to discover what Paul Ciprich had not.

To further complicate matters, the unspecified reward was

bringings the kooks out of the woodwork. One young man bought a dime-store badge and was going around impersonating an officer. He told local residents that he was actively on the trail of Debbie Kline and her abductors, and he even offered police protection to Mrs. Donald Yeager, who was conducting public prayer services for the missing girl. His companion, a sullen young man who would not meet Mrs. Yeager's gaze, claimed to be a Maryland state policeman on inactive duty to investigate the Kline case.

Another odd incident involved a man who was being held in the State Correctional Institute at Huntington, Pennsylvania, at the time of Debbie's disappearance. Paroled in August, he returned to Waynesboro and earnestly began his search for the missing girl. His hunt ranged from Maryland to Florida, but it turned out to be as fruitless as the others. Eventually he was arrested out of state and returned to Pennsylvania as a parole violator.

The man maintained that he was asked to follow up the Kline case by law-enforcement authorities. The authorities maintained otherwise. Before he was returned to jail, he made a chilling statement to Ken Peiffer.

"To tell you the truth, I don't think she's still alive. There are some sick people out there."

One young man, not a known acquaintance of Debbie's, had an unscheduled talk with police after it became known that he was flashing pictures of the missing girl at a local hangout for teenagers. As it turned out, he was merely trying to impress his friends, but he did a far better job of getting attention from the investigators.

To Paul Ciprich, no lead was too small, no veiled suspicion too outlandish to follow up. After concluding his investigation of the wife beater—whose alibi had proven unshakable—he followed up a report of a suspect who had left the area at about the time of Debbie's disappearance. Reported by his landlord, who described him as a loner and "ungodly quiet," he was traced to

California through the various systems Ciprich had at his disposal and picked up and questioned there. Incredulous at what he considered cavalier treatment, he explained that he often left town on a whim, leaving no forwarding address, and he earnestly explained that he had nothing to do with Debbie Kline.

Further investigation confirmed his story.

The Kline case affected nearly everyone in the area, not only potential suspects momentarily inconvenienced by frustrated investigators.

Two local girls, who bore a marked resemblence to Debbie, changed their hairstyles to avoid embarrassing questions. One cut her hair short; the other decided to adopt the swept-back style then in vogue.

The disguise worked for a while, until Peiffer touched up a photograph of Debbie to the style she had worn while working at the hospital. After the picture appeared in the newspaper, the one girl's identity was again questioned.

She changed the color of her hair.

Fall of 1976 dragged on for the Klines. October in Franklin County was the coldest ever recorded. The summer drought had been ended by a week-long rainfall and subsequent flooding. Jimmy Carter was elected President, and the public attention was focused toward Washington and the change of administration.

But in Waynesboro, Pennsylvania, Deborah Sue Kline was still missing.

In that bleak season, when the frost seemed to creep into their very bones, the Klines kept their vigil, waiting for their daughter to come home. Dick started her car every morning. He wanted it to be ready for her to drive as soon as she returned. He kept hope alive in his heart—perhaps, after all, she *had* gone on a fling, or had eloped with some young man. Young people sometimes got romantic notions about such things, and perhaps Debbie was now ashamed to contact her worried family. Maybe the Christmas holiday would change her mind.

It wasn't a rational hope, he knew, but still it helped to sustain him. Jane set Debbie's place for dinner every night. Her younger brothers and sisters joined her parents for the mournful meal. No one mentioned Debbie's name, but each silently prayed for her safe return.

Shortly before Christmas Ken Peiffer dropped in on the Klines. Although it was unusual for a reporter to be so friendly with his subjects, Peiffer had come to think of the family more as friends than as sources. Indeed, Jane and Dick had come to depend on him and on Bob Cox as their contact with the authorities. The reporters tried to bring along an encouraging story whenever they visited the Klines, but lately it had been increasingly difficult to do so.

Jane met Peiffer at the door. "Come on in. Dick's still at work."

Peiffer couldn't help noticing that Jane Kline's dress didn't fit well. She was still losing weight, and her eyes showed signs of prolonged fatigue. Peiffer felt himself entertaining a morbid thought: His instincts told him that Debbie Kline was no longer alive, and it seemed unusually cruel that her parents should be made to suffer through a long, drawn-out ordeal. If it had been Debbie's time to die, how much better it would have been if she'd perished in a conventional accident, instantly. By now her parents would be coming to terms with their grief.

He pushed this thought from his mind as he stepped over the threshold. It was the Christmas season, after all, and he would try to be of good cheer.

"There are two things I want to ask you about," said Jane Kline. "The first I've got no qualms about. The second . . ." She wearily shrugged her shoulders and turned up the palms of her hands.

Peiffer and Jane sat down to coffee. Her lips set in grim resolution, she pushed a handwritten note across the table to him. He read:

> This is to anyone and everyone who reads this paper. Please help us find our daughter Debbie!
>
> She will soon be gone five months, and in my mind and the mind of my family the horror of that Thursday evening is as fresh as if it were yesterday.
>
> Please sit down and go over in your mind—is there any little information you can give us to help? No matter how small it may seem, it could help us.
>
> With the help of God, friends, and family, we got through Thanksgiving and Debbie's nineteenth birthday. But what a beautiful, wonderful Christmas we could have if we could find our loved one. . . ."

The note went on. Peiffer could hardly bear to read it. A lump rose in his throat as he glanced up at Jane. He knew she had been driven to write it out of a sense of profound helplessness, to relieve her unbearable anxiety.

She noticed his concern. "Is the letter OK? You can change it any way you like to make it better."

"I'll break the arm of the guy who touches it," he said. He meant every word.

Jane nodded. Then, taking a deep breath, she continued.

"Now let's get to the second thing. I hardly know how to put it in words. Promise you won't laugh?"

Peiffer promised, although he could have used a good laugh. The sorrow he felt for Jane and her family weighed on him.

"What do you think of contacting a psychic?"

He was surprised, and it showed in his usually imperturbable face.

"I don't know what else to do. The police are doing everything they can. I know that. And I know they don't like it when we call bugging them about Debbie, although they continue to be understanding. It's just that we can't take this waiting anymore. I'm afraid I'll lose my mind if we don't find out something. Anything would be better than not knowing. Anything at all."

"You must do whatever you think best," said Peiffer. Privately he was skeptical about psychics. He'd interviewed a couple in the Shade Gap area, and they hadn't been impressive.

"We tried to contact one in Boston. He's supposed to be good, but he's not for us. As a matter of fact, we never got to talk to him. His secretary told us he would take the case for $1,000 a day—win, lose, or draw. We'd have hired him, but that much money is out of the question."

Peiffer nodded. Silently he was cursing the man who had been so callous with the Klines.

"So then I wrote to a woman in New Jersey who specializes in finding lost children. You have to go through her police department. They screen out the nutty calls."

Peiffer nodded. He knew all about nutty calls.

"Her name is Dorothy Allison."

Part 2

SUSPICION

ONE

Beauty and the Beast

Ronald Henninger crouched down behind his wife's Mercury Cougar and began to unbolt her license plates. He grimaced when he looked back at the mobile home and saw her face in the window. He wasn't the least bit surprised when the door burst open and Barbara came running out.

"Where do you think you're goin'!" she demanded. She had been married to Ron for only a few months, but it seemed more like years. Her life had turned into a series of unending confrontations and arguments—and it now appeared that the marriage was about to end.

"I'll be back Sunday night or Monday," Henninger growled. He cursed as the screwdriver slipped. "I gotta collect something someone has owed me for a long time."

Barbara put her hands on her hips and eyed the husband who

was rapidly becoming a stranger to her.

"Oh really?" she said sarcastically. "If you're only going for a couple of days, then why did you pack all your clothes?"

And she had noticed his guitar and amplifier in the back seat —his prized possessions. Henninger had dreams about becoming a country-western singer, although as far as Barbara could see, most of his ambition had been dissipated in talk and drunken bragging.

She turned and saw her daughter standing in the doorway. Candy Jo's face was streaked with tears. She watched her stepfather and mother as they argued. Ron angrily threw one of the license plates to the ground, then picked it up and walked over to his own car.

The last few hours had been tough on Candy Jo. But now, seeing that her tormentor was about to leave, she was glad she had finally told her mother about what had happened. After Candy Jo made her confession, Ron and her mother had had a terrible fight. And now that look in his eyes! So wild and hateful.

Candy Jo hoped he would never come back.

Barbara started to say something to him when he stood up abruptly, silencing her. The way he palmed the screwdriver was ominous, and she backed away, frightened. Ron looked at her, then tossed the tool contemptuously into the trunk of his car.

His wife leaped out of the way as he jammed the racing engine into reverse. Tires howled and stones flew as he gunned the powerful motor. And then, in a final screech of rubber and a clash of gears, he was gone.

Barbara hugged her daughter.

"What should I do now, Candy Jo? What should I do?"

The policeman who responded to Barbara Henninger's call was curious as he pulled up in front of the ramshackle trailer that hot August afternoon. He remembered the Henningers, and he remembered how the story of the wild young girl who had been run through the car wash to sober up had been passed around the station.

It had seemed like an amusing incident at the time. Now other implications had arisen. When Barbara Henninger admitted him into the trailer, he was taken aback to find another young couple there. She hadn't mentioned company over the telephone.

"This is Rich Dodson and his wife, Lorrie," she explained. "They come over to keep me company. Ron, my husband, the one I called about—he's Lorrie's father."

The officer took a moment to digest this information. Perhaps the incident was more ingrown than he'd originally expected. Rich Dodson stood up and shook his hand. He was a pleasant enough looking fellow, with light hair and long, carefully trimmed sideburns. His wife, Lorrie, smiled. She was quite young, he noted, not more than eighteen. Her long brown hair matched her eyes. He remembered Henninger as an owlish-looking man with thinning hair, and he was a little surprised to be told this attractive young woman was his daughter.

"Where's Candy Jo?" asked the officer.

"In her room. She's real upset right now."

He pulled out his notebook and directed Barbara to begin her story.

"We were in a couple of days ago, about that assault on Candy Jo. I guess you remember that. Well, I just found out Candy Jo didn't tell the whole truth. When I came home that day I found her in bed with only her underpants on. She was drunk, and what she said didn't make a whole lot of sense. That's when I got her and Ron to go down to headquarters. But I just found out she was assaulted that same day by some of Ron's friends." She paused, looking toward her daughter's closed door. "And she was also molested by Ron. He raped her."

The officer looked at Ron Henninger's daughter, Lorrie. She

was staring at the floor. Her husband avoided his eyes.

"When I confronted Ron about it this morning, he grabbed me by the throat and threatened to kill me if I told his parole officer," said Barbara, her voice rising. "I think maybe he's run off to Peoria. Somebody there owes him money."

"We'll have to continue this down at headquarters, if you don't mind," said the officer. He was itching to get back and pull the files on Ron Henninger. "Can you come down tomorrow afternoon? And make sure Candy Jo is along. We'll have to question her."

Dodson spoke up. "Lorrie and I can bring her down. Ron took the plates off her car. She can't drive until we get her new ones."

The officer snapped his notebook shut and got up to leave. Behind the closed door he heard a young girl weeping.

Officer Harold Benchoff had done a little research. Ronald Henninger had managed to put together an impressive record in his thirty-eight years.

It began, so far as the authorities knew, in November 1956, when Henninger was arrested in Bloomington, Illinois, as AWOL from the Navy. He and the Navy apparently did not get along, because he went AWOL seven more times before he was dishonorably discharged.

He managed to stay out of court for three years before being arrested for nonsupport of his wife and children in August 1960. So far, Benchoff noted, he had been no more than a loser, inclined to making trouble and getting himself into situations he was unwilling to accept.

But in November 1960 things began to go sour. He was charged with writing fraudulent checks and forgery. On January 13, 1961, he was again picked up for forgery and sentenced to two to four years at Joliet Prison. Additional forgery charges from Pontiac, Illinois, brought a concurrent sentence of two to four years.

Henninger was paroled in January 1964. And he decided to live it up. He thought he could beat the system, and for several years he did, more or less.

In June of that year he was held by U.S. postal authorities in Peoria. A year later the Bloomington police again picked him up, and to add insult to what he considered injury, they proceeded to charge him with two counts of burglary on two consecutive days.

Eight months later he was back on the street and facing charges of theft in Ocala, Florida. A week later he was charged in Sanford, Florida, with receiving stolen property.

In June of that same year, beginning to think he had the legal bureaucracy licked by now, he was picked up in Decatur, Illinois, and charged with illegal possession of liquor. The next day police added a second charge of possession of liquor and unlawful use of weapons in the crime.

The Bloomington police picked him up again in October 1966 and charged him with theft. Henninger was out of action for a while.

But in August 1969 in Louisville, Kentucky, he was charged with grand larceny. He pleaded guilty (he had been caught red-handed) and was sentenced to five years in prison. That November he was also charged with theft of a motor vehicle and sentenced to another five years, to be served concurrently. The Terre Haute police caught up with him at the same time and charged him with stealing another car.

Shortly after Henninger was paroled, in February 1973, he was charged with murder, aggravated assault, fleeing the police, having no driver's license, reckless driving, speeding, and driving through a stop sign.

Benchoff sighed. He could imagine the shooting, the chase, and, after a scuffle, the arrest.

The flight had begun with the rifle-shooting death of Francis "Frank" Fenton. The first trial ended in a hung jury. At the second Henninger made a deal and pleaded guilty to involuntary manslaughter. He was sentenced to three to ten years in Joliet Prison. In 1975 he was transferred to Vienna Prison, and there, on April Fool's Day 1976, he was paroled.

A genuine April Fool, thought Benchoff. Just then Officer Richard Johnson leaned in to say that Barbara Henninger and her daughter Candy Jo had arrived.

"Show them in," said Benchoff wearily. He knew that sooner or later he'd have to do a lot of paperwork on Ronald Henninger.

Barbara Henninger was nervous. She chain-smoked and glanced at the gold watch on her slender wrist. Her daughter, Benchoff noticed, was more than just pretty. Her creamy complexion was accented by long dark hair that fell below her shoulders. She had a model's figure, accentuated by skin-tight jeans and a clinging sweater. She was only fourteen—but fourteen going on thirty-five, he thought ruefully.

Candy Jo was hesitant at first, but eventually Benchoff was able to calm her down, and she began to recount the incident in vivid detail, and in language that surprised even the officers.

". . . after they ran me through the car wash to sober me up the other day, I went home. I went into my room and took off all of my clothes, except my panties. I was still soaking wet."

She looked up at her mother, who continued to puff on her cigarette.

"And then what happened, Candy Jo?"

"Ron came into the room. He was naked, and he made me have sex with him." Candy shifted her long legs and looked boldly at Benchoff. He sensed that she was relieved to be telling someone, and that beneath her woman's physique she was even more immature than her fourteen years.

"Is that the only time he took advantage of you?"

"No." Candy looked once more to her mother. Barbara nodded, indicating that she should continue.

"Tell us about the other times," Officer Johnson directed. He glanced at Benchoff, who was taking notes.

"The next day Ron took me fishing. I got tired and lay down in the back seat of mom's car. He came up after a while and started to talk. He asked me if I was his lover. I said, "No, I'm your daughter," but that didn't stop him. He started to feel my legs and all. But when I said he'd better stop or I'd put up a fuss, he did."

"Then we went home and I went into my bedroom to get away from him. He came in and started to feel me here." Candy Jo indicated her ample breasts. "He asked me 'ain't you in the mood?' and I said, 'Never with you.'"

Candy Jo hesitated. Benchoff and Johnson waited. Barbara lit another cigarette.

"Then the next afternoon he came into my bedroom and demanded I take three sleeping pills. I got the pills from the doctor when I spilled some hot coffee on my stomach. I couldn't sleep because of the pain."

"Go ahead, you're doing fine," Johnson urged.

"Well, he told me if I didn't take the pills, he would 'break my fucking head.' So I took the pills. They hit me pretty hard, and when I woke up about an hour later, he was lying naked on top of me." She started to sob. Her mother was looking at the floor, her expression wooden and neutral. "Then the next afternoon I was tired and went to bed and he came in again and told me to move over so he could 'love me up.' I started to cry and he got mad and left. That's all."

"That's enough," said Johnson. He turned to Barbara. "Did you know what was going on? Did you know your husband was having sex with your daughter?"

"Yes," she admitted. Her voice was flat, without intonation. A wreath of smoke rose from her cigarette.

"Why did you wait so long to tell us?"

She shifted uncomfortably in her seat and then looked the policeman in the eye.

"I was deadly afraid of what he'd do if we did," she said. "He came into the tavern where I worked the night he left and threatened me if I told anybody. He can be pretty violent. He killed a man, you know."

"We know," said Benchoff. "I've got his record right here. Is there anything else you can tell us about Ron?"

Barbara shrugged. "Lorrie and Richard are outside waiting to take us home. Maybe Lorrie could tell you something."

Benchoff went out to the waiting car and asked Lorrie if she would mind answering some questions. Her husband stayed in the car, listening to the radio.

Lorrie glanced at Barbara and Candy Jo. She wondered just what they had told the police. She took a seat next to Candy Jo and borrowed a cigarette from her stepmother.

"Candy Jo has told us that your father sexually assaulted her. Do you know of any other incidents like that?"

Lorrie examined her nails and looked doubtfully at the policeman.

"Why do you want to know?" she asked. "What do you plan to do with such information?"

"Obviously, we want to arrest him. He's killed a man, he thinks nothing of raping his stepdaughter and threatening his wife's life. He's dangerous. But Candy Jo is only fourteen, and we'd like to shield her identity."

He waited. Watching Lorrie's eyes, he instinctively knew what she was about to tell him.

"Candy Jo wasn't the only one he raped," she declared. "He raped me."

"Can you tell us about it?"

Lorrie hesitated a moment, then nodded. "OK. I'll tell you,

but I won't press charges. He also threatened to kill me."

"That's OK," coaxed Benchoff. "Just tell us the story. We'll give you police protection."

"It happened out at the farm. The Bingaman farm. Richard and I live there with his parents, Mr. and Mrs. Bingaman. It happened shortly after I got there. My dad was visiting for a while. This was just after he got out of prison. Before he got married to Barbara and moved into her trailer." She glanced at Barbara Henninger, who looked away. "Looking back, I guess my father made the first pass at me the day I got there. He was very 'loving,' if you know what I mean. It wasn't like an open pass. I guess maybe anyone else would think it looked like a father-daughter reunion. But it was strange, like he pawed at me where fathers shouldn't."

Once she began, the words began to gush out in earnest.

"I never had a loving, real father like everybody else. I was five years old when we kids, my sister Kathy and two brothers, Kenny and Randy, we were all sent to foster homes. I'm the oldest, and we're all one year apart. Dad was in and out of prison all the time, and I never really saw him until I was in my mid-teens."

"I used to go visit him when he was in the Vienna prison," she continued. "I thought it was the right thing. That's where I met Richard, my husband. He and my dad were cellmates." She glanced nervously at the door. Outside, her husband was still waiting.

Benchoff looked at Johnson. The incident was becoming more incestuous with each revelation.

"Anyway, when Richard and I came to stay at his parents, my dad tagged along. It was the first time I'd really seen him outside of prison. The next day he got me to drink some liquor and gave me some pills. He said they'd make me high and we could talk like a real father and daughter. They were downers, I guess, and when I got real groggy, he started fooling around with me. It was like he was a different person, not my dad. Finally he held me down and raped me. I was scared of him, but I didn't know what to do. I didn't want Richard to find out."

Once more she looked to the door. "It happened more than once," she added.

"Is there anyone who actually saw him taking advantage of you?" asked Benchoff. Lorrie was visibly upset, but he wanted the whole story. Maybe they'd be able to put Henninger away for good this time.

"Yes. Richard's parents. They came into the house one day and found him on top of me. I was crying. Wilbur, that's Richard's stepfather, pulled him off of me and there was a heck of a row. I thought somebody was going to get killed. My father said he'd kill all of us if they told anyone."

"Thanks, Lorrie. I know this hasn't been easy for you."

They got up to leave. Barbara was pale and her hands trembled.

"Candy Jo and I are moving out to the Bingaman farm," she told the officers. We think it's better if we all stick together, and Wilbur Bingaman said he'd be pleased to have us. We're afraid of Ron. If he comes back, I just know he'll try to kill us all. We'll be better protected if we stick together."

Benchoff walked them to the car.

"Don't worry," he said. "We'll keep an eye on the Bingaman place. If Ron shows his face around here, we'll get him."

When he returned, Johnson was straightening out the notes. They conferred and agreed to seek a warrant charging Richard Henninger with rape, indecent assault, corruption of minors, and making terrorist threats.

"Isn't this the messiest thing you've ever heard of?" asked Benchoff.

"It's hard to know who's raping who without a scorecard," agreed Johnson.

"And just for the hell of it," said Benchoff, "let's get a rap sheet on Richard Dodson. He must have known what was going on. After all, he and Henninger were cellmates in Vienna."

TWO

December 1976

Dorothy stood at the stove in her kitchen in Nutley, New Jersey. She was turning sausages.

"Come in, Sal," she called out almost before the knock sounded on her door.

Dorothy Allison was a psychic, but she wasn't using her powers at that moment. Detective Sal Lubertazzi and his wife, Phyllis, were expected, as they were nearly everyday. The Lubertazzis were old friends and more. They worked closely with Dorothy, handling her voluminous mail, a never-ending flow of calls for help. Over the past five years Sal had recorded more than 7,000 of these pleas—some frivolous, but mostly desperate cries for aid in finding loved ones. Many came from anguished parents.

Mrs. Allison looked like any cheerful suburban housewife,

turning from her cooking to greet friends. Sal shut the door quickly behind them.

"Cold out there," he said, shivering a little in the cold December air.

A picture formed in Dorothy's mind. Sal had a message for her—something about a missing person. He slipped the piece of paper to her without a word.

"Dear Detective Lubertazzi," she read:

I read in a newspaper about Mrs. Dorothy Allison helping you with a case in 1975. She helped find two children. I was wondering if you could please help me get in touch with her to help me find my daughter.

She has been gone since July 22, 1976. Our police can't find anything. It will soon be five months, and I and my family are nearly out of our minds.

Her name is Debbie Kline. She was nineteen on November 28. She disappeared coming home from work. We found her new 1976 Vega parked in the mud and thick bushes. Her pocketbook and all her ID cards were in her billfold, along with $30.

Please help me if you can. I don't know what else we can do. Please call me collect anytime.

Please do not think this is a prank or anything like that.

Please, please help me. I have no place else to turn, and it is terrible when you try and try and find nothing. Please help as soon as possible.

Thank you very very much.

Mrs. Richard Kline, Sr.

P.S.: Enclosed is a clipping from our paper. Please help.

Mrs. Allison said nothing when she had finished. She glanced at the clipping. Sal watched as a slight change came over her face, an almost unnoticeable focus of concentration and intensity.

Pictures had come to Dorothy Allison.

Dorothy Allison was only a teenager when her dying mother taught her how to understand rather than fear the unique powers she had inherited. Dorothy was the eleventh child of an Italian family of thirteen, and like her mother, Dorothy "saw" pictures.

Until she was fourteen the "pictures" had been a game, a plaything with which she amused herself and friends. She considered them simply imagination, not knowing that her imagination was radically different from others.

Then one day, leaving her house, she turned back and saw a funeral wreath on the door—a wreath that wasn't really there. Three days later, her father died. Dorothy hadn't even known he was sick. She was disturbed; her uncanny powers seemed to her to be some "evil thing" that had been cast upon her.

Her mother's dying words had calmed her and had made her understand that her gift could be used for good. But it was many years before she put her ability to serious use. While raising her four children, she sometimes did readings for people, but she had never particularly liked it. Somehow it seemed dangerous.

Without warning, her dramatic career began with a nightmare on December 3, 1968. That night she dreamed of a little blonde, blue-eyed boy in a green snowsuit with his shoes on the wrong feet. In the dream he had drowned in a pond, his body wedged in a drain pipe. Looking around the body she saw a gray building, a school, and a door with gold letters on it.

The dream frightened her into calling all her friends and relatives to be sure that their children were safe. When the local paper reported a five-year-old boy missing, Dorothy went to the police. The police were stunned by the accuracy of her description of the missing boy, because it had not been made public. They took her on a search of the Nutley area but were unable to find the site she envisioned—a hill with water on both sides.

A month later the body was discovered in the neighboring town of Clifton, where it had been carried by a stream. The boy was dressed as she had seen him. His body was wedged in a drain pipe in a pond separated from a larger pond by a rise of land. In the surrounding landscape was a gray garage, a schoolhouse, and a factory with gold lettering on the door. And the child's shoes were on the wrong feet.

For a while Dorothy hesitated, trying to ignore her power. She suffered from a vivid horror of the pictures that flashed into her mind like film clips, often rapid and seemingly unconnected, even to herself. She saw victims, their killers, and places where bodies were to be found. She sensed the whereabouts and even the histories and personalities of the murderers.

Not until 1973 did she plunge into police work full time, prompted by the anguish of an hysterical mother. Dorothy reasoned that her gift had to be put to use, that it was a force that might, in the end, accomplish good.

By the time Jane Kline sought her out, she had aided police in more than 100 cases. Among her most cherished possessions were four medals signifying honorary membership in those police departments. And more than one case bore a marked resemblance to Debbie Kline's disappearance.

Four days after Patty Hearst disappeared, Randolph Hearst called Mrs. Allison and asked her to help search for his daughter. Dorothy sensed her presence in Pennsylvania and was able to describe the farmhouse where she was indeed hidden. When the authorities located the house, they discovered they had missed Patty by just a few days. A similar frustration occurred in New York. Mrs. Allison did not succeed in finding Patty Hearst, but her predictions provided some comfort for the family. She told the Hearsts that Patty would be recovered alive and well, and she accurately predicted that she would dye her hair red and travel freely across the country; and also that she would escape unharmed from a fire at which shooting would occur.

Mrs. Allison was not able to provide the same assurance when she was called in to help Union City, New Jersey, police find a missing brother and sister. Immediately she sensed that the eleven-year-old girl had been raped and drowned and that her nine-year-old brother had also been killed. She led police to the bodies after taking them to a cemetery she sensed was important. The cemetery was a false lead and indicative of the time warp from which her pictures often emerge. Past, present, and future appear in the same continuum, and while sometimes Dorothy herself can separate the chronology, often it is up to the police to do so.

Both children were later buried in the cemetery where Dorothy had sought them.

A distraught father approached Mrs. Allison for help. His eighteen-year-old daughter was missing. Dorothy was able to immediately tell him that his daughter was safe, that she had run away, and that the man would become a grandfather. She was able to pinpoint the house where the girl was hidden, and she predicted the day when father and daughter would meet again. When that day arrived, Dorothy refused to accompany the man, saying she did not want to be involved in an accident. The impatient father refused to wait and started out without her.

En route, another car skidded and plowed into his. There were no injuries, and Mrs. Allison accompanied him the following day. The girl was indeed pregnant and had conceived after Mrs. Allison's prediction. And when she showed reluctance to return to her father's home, the Allisons continued to aid the family by offering their own home. The girl remained with them until a reconciliation was effected, and she joined the father of her child to build a family of her own.

In addition to finding missing persons, or their bodies, Mrs. Allison also proved helpful in leading the police to killers. When a child was found raped and murdered in the woods of New Jersey, Dorothy was able to come up with the first name and the occupation of the perpetrator; she also identified a half-dozen other child molesters in the area.

It was natural that Jane Kline would seek out the famed and compassionate psychic, and natural that Sal Lubertazzi, who screened out all but the most urgent requests, would pass Mrs. Kline's letter to Dorothy.

The Lubertazzis chatted with Robert Allison, Dorothy's husband, while the psychic prepared dinner. She loved to cook, and it was not until they had all finished a hearty Italian meal that she alluded to the Klines.

"I'm going to Waynesboro. Maybe before Christmas. I can find their daughter for them."

THREE

At the Bingaman Farm

Barbara Henninger and her daughter, Candy Jo, hurriedly picked up their belongings at the trailer, and before dark they were relocated at the Bingaman's farmhouse. Both felt safer at the farm. They were protected by the Bingamans, who had seen a lot of trouble and took it stoically, and by Richard, who vowed he'd never let Henninger set foot in the house. Two loaded rifles were always in reach.

The women sat in the darkened living room, talking quietly about Henninger.

"He came over here after he left you, you know," Lorrie told Barbara. "He came with his bags all packed and ready to go."

"Why on earth would he come out here?" wondered Barbara. The more she learned about the man she had so recently married, the more she realized she knew very little about him.

"He came to get me," said Lorrie. "He wanted me to come along with him."

"Did he say where he was going?"

"Yeah. He said he was going back to collect a debt, back to Illinois. He was running scared. Maybe he knew you were going to charge him for messing around with Candy Jo. But he was furious about something. He even scared Richard—and he's not easy to scare."

"I'm beginning to think he's crazy," said Barbara, sounding troubled. "I hope to God he doesn't come back here."

"He told me he'd be back tonight or Monday, in time for work. But I don't believe it. In fact, I called him a liar when he said it. I saw that old guitar in his backseat, and I figured he was taking off for good. I felt like if I went along with him, I might never come back, you know?"

The women nodded. Henninger had succeeded in terrifying the household.

"When he told me he was going back to Illinois to collect the money that was due him, it all fit," said Lorrie. "That guy he shot in Bloomington, that wasn't manslaughter. It was murder. He told me so. He even bragged about it. He was going back to collect the money he was paid to do it."

Candy Jo gasped. "Who was the guy?" she asked.

"Frank Fenton. Dad told me he did it for a guy but never got paid because he got caught right away. I didn't know if I should believe him at the time. But I do now. It all fits. There was a trial, but they had a hung jury and dad copped a plea and got three years for manslaughter."

"God!" Candy Jo exclaimed. And to think a cold-blooded murderer had been threatening her.

Lorrie was just beginning to warm up. She felt safe talking about her father, and it was as though she needed to, as though talking relieved some pressure deep within her. The women kept glancing at the windows as she spoke.

"When I told him I knew he was lying about coming back, he just grinned. It kind of scared me, that grin. Then he told me whatever he was going to do was because he loved me and wanted me. He kept pressing me to go with him, but I wouldn't go. I told him I wouldn't because of my husband and family."

Lorrie looked over at Mrs. Bingaman. They had welcomed her into their home, and she was grateful for it.

"I told him I'd finally found someone who loved me, and I wasn't about to up and leave him. But I felt bad, you know, and I begged him not to go because he'd get thrown back in jail for breaking his parole. I told him he didn't have enough money to get to Illinois. 'I'll get it when I get there' is what he said. You know, in that growly voice of his. 'I'll get it when I get there, or else. I'll do whatever I have to in order to collect what is owed me.' "

"That's when he told me to send Richard out. I guess he finally got the message I wasn't going along. He was just staring at me with those scary eyes of his. Then Richard went out and they talked. Richard won't tell me what they talked about, but they sure had a hell of an argument. Ron was yelling and going on and when Richard came in, he was white as a sheet."

It was quiet in the room for a while. Darkness had completely fallen, and the sound of night birds drifted into the room. Finally Mrs. Bingaman broke the silence.

"I only wish I'd never invited that man into my home," she said. "At the time I thought I was doing the right thing. Oh, I know he's your father, Lorrie, and you must feel some kind of kinship to him, but if I had it to do over, I never would have fibbed to the parole people."

"What do you mean?" asked Lorrie. Candy Jo was staring at Mrs. Bingaman with wide eyes. For once she had stopped fidgeting in her seat. In front of the older woman, she seemed self-conscious about her thin sweater.

"Richard asked me to tell the parole people that Ron was his stepbrother. Otherwise they wouldn't have released him. They wanted to have some place for him to go, some family. Otherwise he'd still be in prison. I found out later his own parents back in Illinois wouldn't accept him. They turned the parole people down flat. That should tell you something about the kind of man Ron Henninger is."

Barbara muttered something under her breath. Candy Jo clung to her. Everytime she closed her eyes she could see Ron's face before her, that horrible grin.

"I guess his parents knew him better than Richard did," Mrs. Bingaman sighed. "Ron had him believing tall stories about how people misunderstood him and all. That's why I took pity on him myself. I just figured he had no kin and needed a place to stay for a while. But ever since he came down here, there's been nothing but trouble. The drinking and the drugs and all. And I never dreamed a man would rape his own daughter. Oh, I wish I'd never let that man into my house. And if he'd never come here, he'd never have met you, Barbara. I don't know how he sweet-talked you into getting married so quick, but I do know the man was a slick talker."

Barbara nodded. He sure as hell was. He had come along just when she needed someone, implying that he would help her raise Candy Jo. I'll take care of her just like I'd care for my own daughter, he had promised.

And so he had.

"Well, we'll just have to sit tight and see what happens," said Mrs. Bingaman. "And hope everything works out right."

A few moments later the telephone rang, shattering the tense silence. It rang again. Lorrie recovered herself and slowly lifted the receiver. She was afraid it might be her father.

"Hello," she said, barely audible.

"Lorrie? Is that you?"

It was her grandmother, Marge Baxter, calling from Peoria.

"Grandma!" Lorrie exclaimed happily. "Yes, it's me."

"Honey, I just called to see if you know where Ron is. He left a note at work for me, saying he'd be around."

"When was that?" she asked. If her father wasn't in Peoria, where was he? She glanced at the windows.

"Earlier today. The note said something was wrong with your grandpa. The people who gave me the note said the caller was Ronnie. I thought he was down there with you in Greencastle. Thank heavens the note was a hoax. Your grandpa is OK and sends his love."

"Listen, Grandma. He's got himself into trouble again. He left here a few days ago and said he was going home."

"Wait a minute, dear, someone's at the door."

Lorrie listened as her grandmother put the phone down and walked to the door. She could hear her footsteps echoing through the static of the line. When she picked up the telephone again, Lorrie could hear a voice in the background. A familiar voice.

A chill went up her spine.

"Just answer this yes or no, Grandma," she whispered. "Is that my father?"

"Yes," said her grandmother, assuming a cheerful tone of voice.

"Does he want something?"

"Yes," her grandmother replied.

"Listen carefully. If it's just money, give it to him and get him out of there. I've never seen him in a mood like when he left here. Just give him whatever it is he wants and make him leave. Don't argue with him. I believe he's capable of *anything,* do you understand? I'll let you go now. For God's sake, don't let him know it's me talking to you. I'll call you back tomorrow. Be careful."

She hung up and cast a meaningful glance to the others, who had gathered around her in the darkness.

"You heard it," she said. "He's in Peoria right now."

A sigh of relief went up. Now they wouldn't have to continue the vigil. The night was no longer so threatening. Ron Henninger was hundreds of miles away.

FOUR

December 1976
Waynesboro, Pennsylvania

It was early evening at the *Record Herald*. Most of the staff had gone and the room was quiet, except for the rhythmic tapping of one typewriter. Bob Cox was catching up on some unfinished work. He didn't look up when Ken Peiffer stopped by his desk. He knew what Peiffer wanted—company.

"Forget it," he said. "I'm not going. You know how I feel about mystical types."

Peiffer had told him of the Klines' efforts to contact Dorothy Allison, and he knew the psychic had promised to call that night.

"Has she agreed to help?" he asked, trying to be polite. He liked the Klines and didn't want to see them hurt. There was no telling what sort of nonsense a psychic could come up with.

"Apparently she has," said Peiffer. He was not as skeptical as Cox, but he had his own misgivings. Nevertheless, he had promised the Klines he would be there. "She may appear in person soon. But she says it's not a good time to fly, so she wants the Klines to give her husband directions."

"Her husband?"

"She has no sense of direction herself. Claims she gets lost in her own town."

Cox snorted and looked up from his typewriter. "Sounds great. A psychic who can't find her way around her own backyard. But she's ready to come down here to a town she's never seen and find a girl she's never met, after every cop in the area has been searching for months."

Peiffer shrugged. "Well, as I see it, she can't do any worse. And to the Klines, she's their last hope."

It was nearly ten o'clock when Peiffer arrived.

"You cut things close, don't you," observed Debbie's grandmother testily, tapping her watch. The family sat clustered around the telephone, waiting. "I gave Debbie a watch just like this," continued her grandmother softly as she touched the bracelet of her Timex. "But hers was gold; she doesn't like silver. It was a graduation present." Peiffer wished again that Cox had accompanied him. Just then the phone rang.

Mrs. Kline listened eagerly as Dorothy Allison told her she would be coming to the area, possibly before Christmas.

"That's wonderful!" cried Jane. "But there's something I have to tell you. We're not wealthy and couldn't afford to pay you too much."

"Now you listen to me," Mrs. Allison said firmly. "Your money is no good. I don't want it. I won't take it. And furthermore, if you mention it again, even suggest it, I won't come down. Is that understood?"

"But how can you afford . . . ?"

Mrs. Allison cut her off. "Put the reporter on. Our conversation is ended."

"Can you imagine that woman?" the psychic said to Peiffer.

"All the suffering she has gone through and she expects me to take payment. What kind of woman does she think I am that I would think of taking money for someone's suffering? Well, can you tell me anything new about the case, other than what I read in the article she sent?"

"I wish there was something new," said Peiffer. "But the police are as baffled as ever."

Dorothy did not seem surprised. "Let me tell you what I feel about this case from what I learned in the article and from talking to Jane. I see two people involved."

"Their names are Ronald and Robert or Richard, I'm not sure of the second one. But it will come to me. I see one of their last names as having double letters in it. Maybe it's a middle name, or even both a middle and a last name. I'm not sure of that either.

"One of the men has a knife. He keeps it hidden. One of them lives on a dead-end road. There is a sign there that says "Dead End." They hate each other now, but they had been pals for a couple of years.

"There should be a high hill. That is important. And I see a line of some kind. I'm not sure what kind of line yet, though.

"One of the men is going to get in trouble with the police in late December or January. The other one got in trouble with the police in late July or August.

"One of the guys has someone pregnant right now. I see boots. The one connected with boots was in trouble in Florida some years ago."

"That should give you something to work with for a while, at least until I get down there. I told Jane I would be down before Christmas, and I want to, but I will not fly until after December. Maybe we could take the car. If you have anything else to tell me, call."

"My God," said Peiffer in amazement when he hung up. "I was either just given the biggest snow job in the world, or that woman has something." He looked at the slips of paper he had scribbled on madly as she spoke.

"Did she say anything about Debbie?" Mrs. Kline asked anxiously.

"No. I don't think so. I'm not sure just what she said. I'll have to wait till my head stops spinning."

Peiffer and the family all poured over the notes. None of it made any sense to them. They all knew lots of people with double letters in their names, lots of Ronalds, Richards, and Roberts, lots of people who carried knives of some sort. There was a high hill behind the Kline house.

"I know she'll find Debbie for us," Jane concluded after they all agreed to give up in confusion. "I just have that feeling." But then she began to cry.

"It's too late," she sobbed.

FIVE

Leave-taking, September 1976

Lorrie Lee Dodson was packing her suitcase. Tears streamed down her cheeks. It seemed she was always packing her suitcase. But today her leave-taking hurt more than all the other separations she'd had to endure.

Lorrie had been married to Richard Dodson for only a few months, and she thought she had finally found the home and security she'd craved for all of her eighteen years. She deserved a little security, a little love, she thought, having drifted for most of her life.

Her parents, the Henningers, had given her up for adoption when she was five years old. It was difficult to keep a family together when the father spent more time in prison than out. For Lorrie, the next years passed in a blur of foster homes. She'd been shunted from one place to another, never actually mistreated, but never loved.

As a young teenager she had been adopted by the Thompsons, Robert Lee and Norma Pearl. Then, like many youngsters with ambiguous backgrounds, she became interested in tracing her roots. Now she wished she never had. And it was not as though Grandma Baxter hadn't warned her.

"You stay away from Ron, Lorrie, if you know what's good for you. He's poison. You got along without him all these years, and you don't need him now."

But Lorrie wanted to know the man who was her father, and she finally located him. He was serving time in Vienna Prison, in Illinois, and his cellmate was Richard Dodson. Visiting her father, trying to establish some kind of relationship with him, she had fallen in love with Richard. He was kind to her and seemed interested in what she thought and did. After he was paroled she had continued to see him, and at the time she thought he'd fallen in love with her. It was a nice feeling, one she'd been deprived of all her life, and so she married him and moved to the Bingaman farm.

Lorrie thought she could start a new life there. She loved Richard, who vowed to reform, and she loved the Bingamans. Then her father showed up, and her world darkened. The Bingamans were horrified by his behavior. After he left, Barbara and Candy Jo moved in. Now, a few short weeks later, her marriage was ending.

As soon as Barbara arrived, Richard seemed to lose interest in his young bride. Lorrie suspected an affair. Maybe he thought he was getting even with Henninger. But he either couldn't or wouldn't explain himself to Lorrie.

"I can't tell you now. But someday I will and you'll understand."

But she didn't understand now. All she knew was that she felt terribly hurt, betrayed. Richard had come storming into her room that morning. His face was a mask of hatred, and she cowered before him.

"You said you would do anything to make me happy." He threw some money at her. His tone was contemptuous. "Well, I want you to leave. Get the hell out of my sight, that's how you can make me happy."

The Bingamans, as always, were kind to her. Lorrie decided she would take a bus to Colorado Springs and see if she could find some people she knew there. Mrs. Bingaman drove her down to the bus station.

"Maybe this is the best thing for you, Lorrie," she said. "Richard has changed since he got out of prison. He's not the son I used to know. Not since he got mixed up with that Henninger man."

Henninger again. Lorrie was beginning to revile her own maiden name. All that was bad in her life seemed to have sprung from her father. After Richard had told her to leave, she called her grandmother.

"Lorrie," Grandma Baxter had warned, "you better watch out for yourself. Ron called me, and he swears he's coming back for you. And he says he's coming back to *get* the guy who got you. He means Richard. I don't know where he was calling from, but he's got a pistol and three thousand dollars he stole from us."

That's what finally clinched it. She had gathered together the few bills her husband had hurled at her, and now she was going to Colorado Springs to start over again. Let Richard and Ron fight it out among themselves.

She was getting the hell out.

SIX

A Reluctant Convert

Peiffer hardly slept that night. Incredibly, it was as though he'd picked up an almost electrical charge of energy, merely from talking over the telephone to the psychic. He had lain awake, staring at the ceiling, trying to put it all together—the pictures and images she had related to him. Two people, double letters, a knife, a dead-end road. What did it all mean?

His excitement was still obvious as he related the experience to Bob Cox the next morning.

"When I was talking to her, I got a feeling I can't really describe. It's like a static charge or something. Here, look at these notes."

Peiffer quickly spread out his scraps of paper on Cox's desk. Cox glanced at them reluctantly, running a hand through his hair.

"Look, Ken," he said. "Remember all of our past experiences

with psychics? They bombed out so badly it got to be a joke."

But he began to review the notes with his partner. When they had both gone over them again, Cox sighed and then grinned at his friend.

"Peiffer, you fit just about all the clues Dorothy Allison gave. Double letters in both names. And you've been connected with the law ever since I can remember. Your house sits up on a hill—on a dead end, no less. You always carry a pen knife, and you're wearing boots right now."

"And your name is Robert," said Peiffer. They both laughed.

The psychic's name did not come up again until Cox was shrugging on his overcoat and preparing to leave the office. Peiffer was on the phone, frantically waving at him to return.

"I want you to tell this again to Bob Cox," he said into the phone. "He's working on the case with me."

"It's Allison," he hissed as he urged the phone on Cox.

"Hello, Bob. I was telling Ken that I saw some more things last night," Mrs. Allison began. "The second guy's name is Richard. Ronald and Richard. Look for doubles in both their names."

She is nothing if not definite, thought Cox.

"One of these guys saw Debbie before they took her. I don't know which one, but she was not a total stranger to him. There's something else. Something tragic happened to one of them not too long ago. It could have been a couple of years, but it's still strong in his mind."

"There were new people who moved into the house of one of these guys at about the time Debbie was taken. She was kidnapped, you know."

Cox found himself nodding, as though his image was visible to her over the line.

"There is something else I haven't figured out yet," she continued. "How do you smother when you're not underground?"

The back of Cox's neck prickled; his hair stood on end. He

mumbled something into the phone and the connection was broken. He shivered.

Peiffer broke into his thoughts. "Satisfied?"

Cox nodded. He looked down and realized the hairs on his arms were standing on end, as though ionized by a static charge.

SEVEN

The First Clue

Patrolman Harold Benchoff was sitting in his office, reviewing some notes made by his chief, Charles Daley. Through the window he could see a patch of the gray sky that had plagued Franklin County for most of the month of October. The rain had knocked down the last of the leaves, and the landscape was depressingly somber.

The notes revealed that a fellow named Mike Wenger had called with information he thought might be pertinent to the Kline case. Wenger was a known alcoholic. He was desperately trying to kick the habit, and he wanted to collect the Kline reward money. Benchoff asked him to come in for questioning.

"I can break this case," he had intoned with bleary-eyed seriousness. "And when I get me that money, I'm going south and straighten up. Hell, that dough could save my life—which is why

I'm risking it spilling the beans to you guys."

"OK, Mike," Chief Daley had cheerfully said. "Spill it then."

Wenger leaned in closer, casting furtive glances at the door behind the chief. Daley was amused, but he waited patiently for the alcoholic to continue.

"You got to check out a guy name of Ron Henninger. He's got this sidekick Dodson. They drink together. I know Henninger, you see. He's a big talker and he talked to me a lot. Bought me a couple of beers, you know. A course that's over and done with now, but Henninger, he told me he used to stop by the Waynesboro hospital to 'enjoy the view.' He said, 'man there are some nice chicks down at that hospital. There's something about those white uniforms that really turns me on.' Henninger has a thing for young chicks, see."

Chief Daley was no longer amused. He knew that Henninger was wanted for sexual assault and parole violation, among other things. The Illinois police had been trying to track him down, but so far it had been like trying to round up a puff of smoke.

"Henninger also bragged about 'wasting' a guy out in Illinois. Didn't seem a bit sorry about it," Wenger continued. He licked his chapped lips and looked hopefully at Daley, seeking approval.

"There's one other thing," he said. "He used to brag all the time about how he was going to set his own stepdaughter up as a whore. He was going to have her working the streets. And she's only a kid."

Benchoff examined the notes doubtfully. Wenger had been packed off and assured that if his information broke the case, he'd be mentioned for the reward. But there were probably dozens of men who enjoyed admiring the nurses at Waynesboro Hospital. And Wenger was a drunk. He might be inclined to exaggerate. On the other hand, this Henninger fellow was proving to be a thoroughly nasty character. If he had raped his own daughter and then tried to turn his stepdaughter out on the street, there was no telling what he was capable of. It might be worth following up.

Just then Benchoff's desk phone rang. Long distance from Tucson, Arizona. It was one of those coincidental calls that made Benchoff think there might be something to the theory of ESP after all.

"Listen, my name is Sharon Louise Ruck. Do you know of a guy by the name of Ron Henninger? He used to be from your part of the world."

The woman's tone was one of irritation. Benchoff hardly noticed. He'd been studying that very name on his notes, and now he was hearing it long distance. Henninger obviously got around.

"Yes, as a matter of fact, I do," said Benchoff. "Why do you ask?"

"I want to find out if he's married to someone in Pennsylvania. You see, we were married just two weeks ago, and I have reason to believe he's already married. I think the son of a bitch is a bigamist."

"Lady, I think you just might be right," said Benchoff, reaching for Henninger's file. "Our records show he was married this last May to a Barbara Jean Test. The license was issued on the 24th, and the marriage was performed by Reverend Donald Warrenfeltz."

Sharon Ruck snorted, stifling another curse. "Well, add this to your files. Ron married me here in Pima County, Arizona. My sister and brother-in-law were witnesses. And there's something else you ought to know."

"Yes? Go on," Benchoff urged.

"He's on his way back to Pennsylvania right now to kill a guy named Richard Dodson. He told me so."

Benchoff had been approached several times by Dodson, who wanted a permit to carry a gun for "protection." He was turned down as a known felon.

"How do you know he's coming back here now?" Benchoff asked.

"Because he just took off from here with my son Wade, who

is only sixteen. I guess Wade thinks Ron is a big deal. He ain't old enough to know when a man is lying. And Ron stole a .25-caliber automatic and a shotgun from my sister."

"Jesus," breathed Benchoff.

"Oh, there's more. He told me he'd soon be loaded with money. He said he was going to stop off in Arkansas to 'knock off' some guy. He said he'd get paid $7,000 for the job," said Henninger's latest wife.

Benchoff's palms were sweating. He thanked the woman for her information and said he would get back to her. He immediately placed a call to Henninger's parole officer. Then he called the Tucson police. One of the officers there said he would check out Sharon Ruck and make sure the call hadn't been some kind of elaborate hoax.

Benchoff didn't think it was—not from what he was getting to know about Ron Henninger.

He called the Interstate Compact in Chicago and informed the probation department of Henninger's latest escapade. By the time this was done, he received a return call from Tucson. They'd checked on Sharon Ruck's story. She was telling the truth.

The police in Bloomington, Illinois, knew Henninger. They had a pretty good idea where he'd eventually show up when he was on the run, and they staked out the Baxter home.

Sure enough, Henninger was picked up there on October 22, 1976. He appeared to be a little sheepish over the incident. He had only a few dollars on him. The guns were found in his trunk. Wade, the sixteen-year-old son of Sharon Ruck, was sent home to his mother. His cross-country adventure was over.

And Ronald Henninger was back in jail.

Lorrie Lee Dodson received word in Colorado Springs that her father had been picked up. With him safely behind bars, at least for the time being, she left for Illinois to stay with Grandma and Grandpa Baxter.

They told her about the numerous attempts her father had made to find her. How he had made late-night calls from god-knows-where, demanding that they tell him where she was. They never did.

Lorrie told them she had gotten a letter from her father while she was in Colorado. The note had been left with a friend. Apparently he had found out that she was in the area, but not exactly where. He wanted Lorrie to come and live with him and his new wife, Sharon, in Tucson. But Lorrie figured the note was sent to flush her out of hiding, to make her run back to Illinois, where he could easily find her. Instead, she second-guessed him and stuck it out.

Back with the Baxters, she got a job as a cocktail waitress. She liked the job, but her thoughts kept returning to Richard Dodson. She had talked with him over the phone, and he said he wanted her back. Barbara and Candy Jo had left the Bingaman farm, and he promised that things would be different between them.

Lorrie decided she would let him sweat for a while, and she stayed in Illinois for two months before returning to the Bingamans.

One incident kept reoccurring to her, like a bad dream. It had taken place at the farm shortly after she and her husband had been married. Her father was there, and trouble had begun. Lorrie warned him that she was going to call his parole officer unless he stopped taking drugs and drinking all the time.

Ron had a beer in one hand and his hunting knife in the other. He had honed the blade to razor sharpness and hid it in his boot. He carried it everywhere he went.

"You got to settle down. You can't keep up like this, drinking and popping pills all the time," Lorrie had pleaded.

There was blood in Henninger's eyes as he glared at his

daughter. He just sat there, wiping his knife on his pants. He looked at Lorrie, then at the knife, then at her again.

The silent message had been unmistakable. Months later the recollection still haunted her.

A few days before Christmas Cox and Peiffer received another call from Dorothy Allison.

"It's snowing to beat the band up here," said the psychic. "I won't be able to get down your way before Christmas, as I'd hoped. I just talked to Jane Kline. I hate to disappoint them, but there isn't much any of us can do about the weather. And after the holidays I've promised to look for the murderer of two children up here. So I won't be down for at least a couple of weeks."

Peiffer said he understood. The snowstorm was raging outside the newspaper building, mounting into a full-scale blizzard.

"By the way, one of the guys who took Debbie was illegitimate. And I'll tell you something else. Debbie is dead. I know that. When I come down there, we will be looking for a body."

Peiffer looked up at Cox, startled. He pulled the phone away from his ear so they could both listen.

"She's dead. I'm positive. But don't tell the Klines. Let them have their holiday."

They hung up the phone. The day had suddenly become grim.

EIGHT

The Undercover Agent

The new year, 1977, came in with a roar, dumping another six inches of snow on Franklin County and blowing the back roads shut with drifts several feet high. The dense wooded areas were frosted with ice. After a brief Christmas respite, winter was definitely upon them.

Lorrie returned to the Bingaman farm on the third of January. As Richard had promised, Barbara and Candy Jo were gone. They had returned to their trailer. Henninger was in jail in Illinois, and they no longer needed the Bingaman's protection.

And Richard had turned over a new leaf. He had gotten a job as a truck driver with a St. Thomas fuel-delivery firm. He told Lorrie that he loved her, that he had loved her all along, that whatever it was that had happened between himself and Barbara was over forever.

That same week Dorothy Allison left frigid New Jersey for Florida. A case there demanded her immediate attention, and the prospect of some time in the hot sun was a welcome bonus. She called the Klines and promised she would be back in two weeks to devote her full time to finding their missing daughter.

Dick Kline had just cleared the snow from the driveway when Paul Ciprich pulled in in an unmarked cruiser. Ciprich was just dropping by. He wished he had something concrete to tell them, but the case seemed hopelessly stalled. All they had were rumors, many of them conflicting.

Jane had his coffee poured by the time he'd taken off his top coat. Ciprich had continued his friendship with the Klines over the months. A close involvement with the family was not the best practice in a case like this, the state trooper knew. Yet he couldn't help himself. You just made friends with the Klines. It was as simple as that.

Neither Jane nor her husband mentioned Dorothy Allison to him. The psychic had become their secret weapon, their last hope, and they didn't want to have anyone—not even Ciprich—discourage them.

Ciprich had barely finished his coffee when the call came in. The county probation officer wanted to talk to him, urgently, about the Kline case.

Debbie's parents heard only one side of the conversation.

"Don't get your hopes up too high. This might not amount to anything," cautioned Ciprich as he saw the glow in their faces.

The trooper threw on his coat and hurried back to the barracks.

"Bruce Arnold!" he exclaimed when the parole officer told him who wanted to talk to him about the case.

Ciprich knew Arnold's background. He was on parole for

assaulting his wife. After taking a bullwhip to her, he'd finished the job by clubbing her with a gun. A rather unsavory character, to say the least.

"This guy's a goofball," said Ciprich. "What in hell does he want?"

"I know he's half-crazy, but he claims he knows who took Debbie Kline," said the parole officer. "I thought you ought to know."

Ciprich nodded, musing on the information. "Thanks. Well, I've talked to a lot of people on this case, and I suppose one more nut isn't going to hurt. Let's go."

He and the parole officer drove over to the Greencastle plant where Bruce Arnold was working. They received reluctant permission to talk to the employee on company time.

Arnold, in his late twenties, was about six feet tall, very slender, and wore a thin mustache, which barely covered his upper lip. He hadn't a tooth in his mouth. Ciprich eyed him suspiciously because Arnold wasn't known for being reliable, and he had an inflated sense of his own importance.

"We'll talk in the car," said Ciprich when he noted that other employees had taken a sudden interest in the confrontation.

"Yeah. Good. It would be safer for me if nobody knew what I'm going to tell you."

Although Arnold had trouble pronouncing certain words, he came straight to the point.

"I know who kidnapped Debbie Kline. It was Rich Dodson and a guy by the name of Ron Henninger. And they killed her too." Excitement rose in his voice.

Ciprich had his notepad out, but he didn't write. For the first time since the twenty-second of July—more than 150 days—he had something he might be able to get his teeth into. Someone had named names.

At the same time he wasn't really prepared to believe Arnold. He looked at the parole officer, who was staring blankly at his charge. The silence in the car was deafening.

"Didn't you hear me?" insisted Bruce Arnold. "I know who took the Kline girl. I got proof."

"OK. Let's start with the proof part," said the trooper skeptically. Dealing with Arnold left a bad taste in his mouth. He could imagine the man's wife, beaten senseless with a bullwhip. The thought disgusted him.

"OK, but you gotta promise me. You gotta let me do this my way. I want to work as an undercover agent on this. I'll set up a meeting with the person who told me, the one person who should know," he demanded.

Ciprich grimaced. He didn't like the idea of Arnold working undercover. It was too much like a cops and robbers game—too much like playing at Dick Tracy. But Bruce Arnold was adamant. Finally Ciprich decided to humor him. He knew from past experience that information often had to be gotten by distasteful methods.

And experience had also taught him that most of the information gained that way was useless. But it was the only thing he had to go on. He signaled Arnold to continue.

"I know the wife of one of the murderers. We met in Greencastle. She works in a bar over that way. You let me set it up and she'll tell you the whole story."

"Do you know anything more than the names?" asked Ciprich. "Do you know any of the circumstances?"

"I sure do," replied Arnold. He leaned forward conspiratorially, bad breath reeking from his toothless mouth. "They took her and they raped her and then they killed her. I even know where they buried her."

"Go ahead," urged Ciprich.

"She's buried in a dump up near Fayetteville." Arnold was glowing, very pleased with himself. Then his smile abruptly faded.

"But I want you to know someone is after me!" he blurted. "The past couple of days someone took a few shots at me right here at the plant." He swept his hand around, indicating the parking lot.

"But I can take care of myself. I was in the Marines, you know. I just ran and ducked the shots. They came pretty close, but as you can see, they missed," he bragged.

Ciprich and the parole officer exchanged glances. Here was a man who claimed he could dodge bullets. Ciprich suppressed a smirk, controlling his irritation when he noticed Arnold wiping his muddy boots on the cruiser's upholstery.

"Where did you get this information?"

"Like I said, from Barbara Henninger. She and I are real good friends, if you know what I mean. She told me all about it," he said importantly. It was obvious to the trooper that Arnold considered himself a real stud, a he-man. A he-man who took a bullwhip to his wife, then pistol-whipped her.

"Will she talk to me?" asked Ciprich.

"Not if she knows you're a cop. That's why I got to go undercover on this. You got to meet us in disguise; then I'm sure she'll talk. I can set it up. I'm seeing her again tonight and I'll set us up a meeting. We'll set down in a bar up in Chambersburg and discuss it over a couple of drinks."

Ciprich said he'd be there. He wondered if Arnold expected him to wear a paste-on mustache.

"That's fine, Mr. Arnold. You can introduce me as Debbie's cousin. Call me Paul. We'll meet at that bar out on Wayne Avenue tomorrow evening. But before you go, give me everything you know, just the way detectives do."

That approach appealed to Bruce Arnold. He puffed out his narrow chest and began to talk excitedly.

"Well, Barb—that's Henninger's wife—she told me that Dodson told her about it. She said when they were living together Dodson would have nightmares and blurt things out about the Kline girl. So Barb told Dodson what she'd heard him say in his sleep. She really laid it on thick, I guess. That's when he confessed to her and all."

"Why did she tell you and not the police?" asked Ciprich.

"She's afraid of Henninger. That's who I think's been takin' shots at me—Ron Henninger." He looked around the parking lot and seemed relieved to be under police protection. He grinned at Ciprich. "That's why you can't tell her you're a cop. Don't lay that on her or she'll clam up."

"OK. Now just remember I'm Debbie's cousin Paul. Now what's this about the girl being buried up near Fayetteville?"

"That's what Dodson told her. He said they buried her in a dump up that way. Maybe she can tell you more."

"Is that all you know?"

"That's all. Maybe undercover I can find out more stuff," said Arnold.

"Fine. You've done the right thing. Now stay loose and get back to me at the barracks when you've set up the meeting."

"I will," said Arnold solemnly. "I'll call you and tell you when. We can synchronize and stuff."

He strutted back to the plant, eyeing the parking lot mysteriously.

"What do you think?" asked the parole officer.

Ciprich shrugged. "I don't know what to think. It might be a tall tale he's made up. Or it might be someone is pulling his leg. Or maybe we're onto something. If this woman I meet tomorrow is really Henninger's wife, and she confirms what he said, then I'll start getting excited. Until then, we'll just have to play along with our 'undercover agent.' "

Back at the barracks, Ciprich reported to Corporal John Farrell, describing the proposed meeting with Henninger's wife.

"I may have to go boozing on company time," Ciprich joked. Then he added soberly, "Maybe this is the break we've been waiting for."

NINE

The Source

Bob Cox was just leaving for work when he got a call from Dorothy Allison. She was in Florida and had received more "pictures" concerning the missing girl. Cox immediately began to take notes.

"One of the guys involved in the Kline case is already in jail," she said. "I'm quite sure of that. I see a prison or a jail. But it's not the Kline case they have him in for, it's something else."

"Do you know who? Which one of the two?" His mind raced. He tried to remember if he'd heard anything about an arrest that would have resulted in the commitment of someone named Ronald or Richard. By now he had tempered his original skepticism. His research into the psychic convinced him she was the genuine article. She might be just the person to break the Kline case.

"Yes. He's the one who committed incest," she replied. "He's an animal. A real animal. He'd rape his own mother if he got the chance. But in this case it was his daughter. He raped his own daughter, and he's raped others."

"I'll get right on it and see if I can find anything," promised the reporter. "When are you planning to come back?"

"I'll be down here five more days. Then I'll get right to work and find the Kline girl. I'll be in Waynesboro next week, so tell her parents not to worry. Things are breaking for the police now, and they won't have to wait much longer. You can tell them something very important happened either yesterday or today. The police are getting close."

She recounted this as calmly as though she had been describing the weather.

Cox rang off and immediately put in a call to the state police barracks. John Farrell answered. Cox remembered him from the William Hollenbaugh manhunt he had recounted in *Deadly Pursuit,* and he figured if anyone knew anything about new developments, John Farrell would.

But Farrell was evasive.

"You didn't slip on the ice and bump your head, did you, Cox? What makes you think we've got new developments?" Farrell was thinking about the meeting Ciprich was about to set up with Barbara Henninger. The last thing he wanted was a reporter botching up their first solid lead. There would be plenty of time to call in the press later, after all the loose ends had been tied up and the culprits were safely behind bars.

"I was just fishing," said Cox lamely.

"Better luck next time," said Farrell, ending the conversation.

Cox put the receiver down slowly. Dorothy Allison was trying to tell them something, but for the life of him, he couldn't figure out what.

Paul Ciprich was cleaning up some aggravating paperwork when he got the call. He glanced at his watch. Bruce Arnold had said the meeting would be in the evening and here it was just 1:30 in the afternoon. But Ciprich had had a good long look at Henninger's rap sheet, and he was disinclined to keep his "undercover agent" waiting.

In less than thirty minutes he had changed his clothes, swapped cars, and driven across town to the bar. He parked his pickup truck beside the only other vehicle in the lot. It was a 1968 Cougar, green with a black vinyl top. He took down the license-plate number and went inside.

It was pitch black inside the bar. At first he thought he was alone, but when his eyes adjusted to the dim light, he saw them in the back room of the tavern, seated at a corner table.

Arnold's cowboy hat took up half of the small table. Seated beside him was an attractive woman with dark hair. To Ciprich they seemed to be an oddly mismatched couple.

"Hello. I'm Paul," he said as he pulled up another chair. The woman was staring at her mixed drink. Bruce Arnold was clutching an empty bottle of beer.

"This here is Barb. Barb, meet Paul," said the undercover cowboy.

"Pleased to meet you," she said. No discernible accent, Ciprich noted.

"Bruce was telling me about you yesterday," said the trooper, trying to open the conversation. She merely nodded and continued to examine her glass. He decided to skip the subtleties.

"Arnold tells me you know who took Debbie Kline."

No reaction. Somebody slipped a coin into the jukebox and a sad country-western tune drifted across the room.

"That's what you told me, right Bruce?" said Ciprich.

The woman studied him, trying to read his face.

"What's your interest in this?" she asked.

"I'm her cousin and I'm trying to find out all I can about her disappearance. Those damn dumb cops aren't getting anywhere," he threw in. That seemed to work. She softened.

"Well, I don't know what he told you," she said, thumbing her companion. "But I can tell you this. You're too late to save her life. She's dead."

Then she looked down at her glass and suggested a refill. Arnold nodded furiously in agreement. Ciprich ordered the first of what would be many rounds. He felt sick and sad inside.

"We took this table so I wouldn't have my back to an open door or window," Arnold explained. "We don't want no one sneaking up on us."

"Good thinking," Ciprich replied. On first impression Barbara Henninger was extremely cool. The trooper wondered what on earth she was doing with a guy like Arnold, and why she'd been telling him secrets.

"What can you tell me about it?" he asked her.

"My husband and another guy took her and did her in," she replied matter-of-factly.

"Do you mind if I take a few notes?" he asked.

"Why not?" she shrugged. She couldn't care less apparently.

Ciprich tried not to make it look too official as he pulled out a small notebook and pen. He flipped the cover over quickly so she wouldn't see his name on it.

"Ron Henninger and Richard Dodson. Those are the boys who did it," she said. "They picked her up, took her into the mountains back of Fayetteville, and raped her. Then Ron slit her throat."

"How do you know this?"

"Richard told me. He used to have nightmares about it and talk in his sleep. One day I asked him about it and he told me." As she talked she kept one eye on the door.

"Where are these guys now?" Ciprich asked, writing feverishly.

"Ronnie's in jail out in Illinois. He got picked up for violating parole and some other things. Richard lives over in Greencastle at the Bingaman farm. Mrs. Bingaman is his mother. He just got a job working for a fuel company over near St. Thomas."

She watched Ciprich writing and stared idly at the table. "Richard used to get those nightmares all the time. He said all he could see was the blood running down the front of her blouse."

Ciprich noticed that her voice was picking up as she recounted the story. He still wondered why she was telling him, a perfect stranger, and why she hadn't gone to the police long before.

"Ron left here last August and he ain't come back. I hope he never does. He never told me about it, the killing, but knowing him as I do, I can believe Richard."

"Ronald is a bad nut. I know for a fact he already murdered one guy out in Illinois," she continued. "That's what he was in prison for before he came out this way. He bragged about it, bragged about shooting the guy down in cold blood. They only got him for manslaughter though. Ron thought that was a great joke. He loves to pull the wool over people's eyes. Especially cops."

Arnold didn't seem too keen about her telling Ciprich about the Fenton killing, and he tried to interrupt and change the subject. Barbara ignored him and focused her attention on Ciprich. He couldn't help wondering if she had guessed he was a cop.

"Richard told me that he and Ron followed the Kline kid from the Waynesboro hospital. They snatched her out of her car, then drove up to this dump. They took turns raping her, and after it was done Ronald slit her throat. Richard used to cry about it all the time."

"Do you know where this dump is?" Ciprich asked casually. He was trying to remain calm, but his heart was thumping.

"Well, Richard once drove me up to Eagle Rock, and he broke down and cried up there, too. But he never did show me the place."

"Do you know if it was a big dump? A public place?"

"I don't think so. I got the idea it was a little place, the kind you see everywhere."

At that moment a friend of Ciprich's walked into the bar. Paul tried to avert his face, but his friend spotted him. Ciprich stood up and met him before he got to the table, and in a terse whisper asked him not to blow his cover. The friend cooperated.

Several rounds of drinks later, Arnold and Barbara departed. Ciprich picked up the tab. The information he received was well worth the price.

Back at the barracks, he reported in to John Farrell.

"We got an inquiry from Bob Cox over at the *Record Herald*," he told Ciprich. "I think he's onto something. Wanted to know if there had been any recent developments."

"How the hell did he know that?" asked Ciprich, incredulous.

Farrell shrugged. "Beats me. He said he was just 'fishing,' but I don't like the sound of it. I want the press out of this until we clean it up. One wrong move and our new sources may dry up."

Ciprich nodded. "So far we've got nothing but hearsay evidence. It will never stand up in court. I doubt we could even get a warrant. We need some hard evidence. We need to locate the body."

"That could be difficult," said Farrell grimly.

"Arnold is coming here again tomorrow."

"We'll both talk to him," Farrell replied.

Ciprich sat down and went over the rap sheet that had just come in on Richard Dodson. It told an unpleasant, ugly story.

He'd first come to the attention of the Franklin County juvenile authorities in 1959, when he was thirteen. He was charged with theft and released in the custody of his parents.

Four years later he was in court again, this time for picking up a thirteen-year-old girl in Hagerstown, Maryland, and bringing her across state lines, where he kept her at his home and the homes of relatives until her worried parents finally located her.

Ciprich mused on that one. You could look at it two ways —either Dodson had been a lovesick boy, or he had carried out his first abduction.

In April 1963 he was again picked up for theft.

As an adult, in 1964, Dodson was twice convicted of disorderly conduct. The next year he was convicted of forgery. All of this took place in the Franklin County courts.

And then, in 1972, at the age of twenty-six, he was charged with the rape of a fourteen-year-old girl. He had married for the second time and had four children. Through plea bargaining in the courts, the rape charge was dismissed, and he pleaded guilty to indecent liberties charges.

Ciprich paused and sucked in his breath. Two days before Dodson was sentenced, his house burned to the ground. His wife and three of his children perished in the fire. His four-year-old boy was severely burned and had been institutionalized in a burn clinic ever since. Dodson, who had been in the house at the time, escaped without a scratch.

Curiouser and curiouser, Ciprich thought. Despite the tragedy, Dodson was sentenced to serve four to six years in the Illinois Correctional Institute. He was later transferred to Vienna Prison, where he shared a cell with Ronald Henninger.

Dodson was paroled on May 24, 1976. Two short months before Deborah Sue Kline disappeared.

Bruce Arnold sauntered into the state barracks as though he belonged there. Ciprich took him to the conference room and notified Farrell. The questioning began in earnest.

"You said you had more to tell us about one of the guys. Which one?"

"Dodson," said Arnold brightly. He explored the conference room with his eyes, assuming an air of importance. "He and me used to go girl hunting. He showed me how easy it was to pick up girls."

"And where did the two of you do this?"

"Well, Dodson and I, I'll call him Rich, because that's what I used to call him, we often took trips together. We would come up to Chambersburg and even to Carlisle, and we'd pick out women and he'd say how a certain woman could be picked up. You just said certain things to them and then if that didn't work, well, he said, 'Just grab 'em and that's it.' That's the way he liked to talk. Then he said how simple it must have been to take the Kline girl—said all the guy would have had to do was just grab her."

"But we never actually grabbed any," he added quickly. "I would never do that."

"Of course you wouldn't," said Ciprich. He then suggested that another investigator join them. Richard Lingenfelter was summoned before Arnold could protest. Arnold went over the highlights of the information he had given Ciprich in the last few days, but it was obvious he didn't care to repeat himself. But when Lingenfelter suggested Arnold submit to a polygraph test, he scarcely hesitated.

"Don't you believe me?" he asked.

"Sure we believe you," Ciprich replied. "But this way, if you pass the test, *everyone* will have to take your word for it."

"That's a fact," Arnold agreed. "Let's have at it."

"Well, it can't be done right this minute. First of all we have to get the polygraph technician in here to operate the equipment and read the tape. That will take a day or two to arrange."

Arnold was disappointed. He obviously liked the idea of taking a lie-detector test. "Well, just tell me when you're ready."

"Arnold, I would like to ask you a question and I don't want you to be offended, is that OK?" Ciprich asked.

"Sure, you won't hurt my feelings."

"There's a large reward for information in the Kline case. You wouldn't be making this all up just to collect the reward?"

"Hell, no!" Bruce Arnold was indignant. He slammed his cowboy hat back on his head and stood up. "I ain't here because of no reward, but if there is one, you can be sure I'll take it. I'm here to tell you who killed Debbie Kline and that's all."

"I think you hit a nerve," said Lingenfelter after Arnold left.

"Clumsy of me," said Ciprich, and they both laughed.

Then Ciprich dialed Kerry Sanders, the state parole officer, and asked him to get everything he could lay his hands on that might apply to Henninger and Dodson.

He had no sooner put the phone down when Bruce Arnold was again standing in front of his desk, his cowboy hat in his hands.

"Buddy, you got to help me out," he told Ciprich. "I'm up at the end of the road, out of gas. Lend me five bucks and I'll see you get it right back."

Ciprich rolled his eyes but forked over the five dollars, drove Arnold to a service station, and helped him restart the green Cougar. Then, on a whim, he decided to drop in on Barbara Henninger.

This time, however, he did not pretend to be Debbie's cousin. He introduced himself as a state policeman. Barbara didn't seem even slightly surprised, and he wondered again if she had ever fallen for Arnold's undercover game.

"I'd like to go over the information you gave me yesterday," he said.

"Sure, why not?"

Once more he heard the story Dodson had related to her. The only new information that she could add was that Dodson had once mentioned the Pines. A store in the Fayetteville area came to the officer's mind.

"You've been a big help. I think we can develop something out of this now. I'll be back to you again soon." Ciprich tipped his hat and backed out the door of the tiny trailer.

"Anytime," she called after him.

Part 3

THE CONFESSION

ONE

January 12, 1977

Lisa Prescott shivered as she peered at the thermostat. She put it up a few notches. Outside, under leaden skies, the weather was bleak and cold. She hoped this most recent cold snap would soon come to an end. The fuel bills had been astronomical.

Lisa wiped away at the frosted window and looked out. Snow was beginning to spit and she shivered again. She thought with a sigh that winter seemed to be lasting forever. A fuel delivery truck pulled to a stop in front of her house. She could hear the throbbing of the heavy engine and see clouds of gray-blue smoke rise from the exhaust. One of the men climbed out of the truck and made his way to her door, kicking at the snow.

She met him at the door.

"I'm new on this route, ma'am, and I can't find the next place

I got to make a delivery. The folks are about out of fuel. Do you mind if I use your phone to call in?"

His face was partially hidden by his heavy coat, but Lisa could see his blond hair and the prominent cheekbones that made his eyes look deeply set.

"Sure. It would be awful to run out on a day like this," she said.

He grabbed her by the arm as the door closed behind him.

"I seen you outside a few days back," he said, pressing his face next to hers. She could smell the beer on his breath. Lisa shrieked and tried to twist away. His fingers tightened in a vise around her arm.

"I seen you and I want you. Scream and I'll break your neck," he said. His voice was thick and vicious.

Lisa felt herself being pushed backward. She opened her mouth and cried out. He shook her again.

"I said I'll break your face. Now shut your trap."

He was dragging her across the living-room floor toward the open bedroom door. She kicked out, hitting nothing but air. One of her hands caught something and a lamp toppled off the bureau.

"My arm! Let go of my arm!" she cried. The pain cut like a hot fire into her shoulder. Her attacker ignored her, his breath heavy. Lisa tried to hook her feet against the doorjamb, but it was useless. He charged on into the bedroom and hurled her on the bed, locking her arms behind her back and pulling her skirt up over her face.

"Quit moving. I aim to fuck you and there's no way around it."

She stopped kicking when he squeezed her arms. It felt as though they might be dislocating at the sockets and she groaned, the pain shooting in flashes behind her eyes. She shook her head, trying to get the skirt out of her face as he pawed at her, spreading her legs.

"I seen you outside and I knowed I wanted you. When you

want something, you just go ahead and take it. Now hold still or I'll break your neck. I swear I'll kill you if you don't hold still."

He had worked his hand under the elastic of her panties, probing her with blunt fingertips. She tried to squirm, her eyes hot with tears. He grunted, there was a tearing sound, and she was naked.

"No!" she cried. "You can't!"

"Shut up telling me I can't. I say I will." He pushed her back down and fumbled with his belt. The sound of the descending zipper terrified her more than the pain, and even more than his miasmic breath against her neck.

"You can't," she sobbed. "I'm having my period. You can't."

"Shit. Well, that ain't stopping me. A little blood never bothered me."

He pried her legs apart again and yanked the tampon out of her. She began to sob, beating her fists against his back as he tried to mount her. He began to push at her horribly, painfully, cursing.

"Damn it!"

Suddenly he rolled off of her and stood up, buttoning his pants.

"You think you ain't getting it, but you will. I'll be back, just wait. I ain't going to be denied. And listen here . . ." He was back down against her, twisting her arm, his open mouth pressed against her ear.

"You tell a soul and I'll kill you, do you hear? I'll slice you open. I'll cut you so bad they won't ever know what you looked like."

And then he was gone.

Lisa got up on all fours, blinded by tears. Her breath came in shuddering convulsions as she crawled to the phone.

Paul Ciprich had been back in the barracks for less than a half-hour when a call came through on an assault and attempted rape. The incident was assigned to Trooper Paul Weachter.

The victim was apparently hysterical and the report garbled. Weachter was putting on his coat, preparing to leave for an investigation. He casually read the report aloud. Ciprich nearly slipped off of his chair.

"Say that again," he asked Weachter.

"I'm going to check out an attempted rape up in the Fort McCord area," the trooper replied.

"No, the part about the truck driver," said Ciprich excitedly.

Weachter read from the report. "Says here the woman was attacked by a man operating a fuel delivery truck. She let him into the house to use the telephone. Said he was new on the job and didn't know the location of the next customer."

"Jesus!" exclaimed Ciprich. "Maybe it's just a coincidence. And maybe not . . ."

"What's gotten into you?" asked Weachter.

"I've got a suspect in the Kline case. He's a convicted rapist. And he just got a job with a fuel company out that way. His name is Richard Dodson."

Ciprich searched through his files and presented Weachter with a photograph of Dodson. It seemed like a long shot, but Weachter put the snapshot in with a number of other pictures he always carried to show crime victims.

Trooper Weachter drove carefully over the snow-covered roads. He had to stop once to clear his windshield. As he turned down the narrow lane that led to the victim's house, he noticed truck-tire tracks in the snow.

Lisa Prescott was an attractive, twenty-six-year-old woman, recently married, but she looked older when she greeted Weachter at the door. Her eyes were red, her face pale, her lips trembling. Her young husband was with her. He had his arm protectively around her shoulder as she described the attack.

Weachter tensed up as she talked. Her description of the would-be rapist fit Dodson.

"See if you can identify any of these men," he asked, handing her the stack of photographs.

She studied each one intently as her husband watched. She was halfway through the stack when she screamed.

"My god! That's him! That's the man!" She tossed the photo back at Weachter, as though she couldn't bear to touch it. It was the snapshot of Dodson. Weachter was afraid she was going to faint. He and her husband helped her to the couch.

"One thing, Mrs. Prescott. Will you testify in court if we catch him? He may confess, and then you won't have to."

Lisa gathered her strength, holding tightly to her worried husband. "Yes," she said emphatically. "Yes. I'll swear to it before judge and jury."

Weachter recovered the photographs and left, thankful that her husband had been able to get there so quickly. If not, Weachter would have been obliged to stay there until another trooper had been summoned. Dodson had sworn he'd be back.

As Weachter pulled his unmarked cruiser out of the Prescott's driveway, he saw something that made him doubt his vision. A fuel truck was passing. It slowed down as it went by the driveway.

The trooper had butterflies in his stomach as he moved from the lane and fell in behind the heavy truck, which took up more than half of the snow-encroached road. It turned left down a narrow back road that led out to the rarely used army depot gate. The snow was deeper here, and Weachter's car began to slip, his wheels spinning.

It's now or never, he thought. He flipped on the siren and the four-way flasher.

The truck slowed but didn't stop, as though expecting him to pass.

Weachter turned on the loudspeaker concealed behind the front grille.

"This is the state police. Pull over and stop your truck!"

The sound echoed across the barren landscape. Weatcher unsnapped the holster of his service pistol. The truck stopped, blocking the road. The driver jumped down out of the cab. He wore a heavy, pile-lined jacket, and as he walked toward the cruiser, both hands were in his pockets.

It was Richard Dodson.

"Stop right there and take your hands out of your pockets!" Weachter commanded over the loudspeaker. They were alone on an isolated road.

Dodson slowly pulled his hands out of his pockets, grinning. He held them in full view as he walked to the passenger's side of the cruiser, opened the door, and got in. Weatcher leveled the pistol at him. He didn't flinch.

"Keep your hands on your knees," said the trooper. He then outlined Lisa Prescott's story, including the assault in the bedroom.

"Sure I stopped there. But that woman is dreaming. I didn't touch her," said Dodson. He was still grinning. It was the full-tooth grin of a shark, and Weachter kept his hand on the pistol.

"She's mistaken," insisted Dodson. "She told you there was someone along in the truck and I'm by myself. See? There ain't nobody in that cab."

Weachter glared. "She positively identified you from a photograph. This one right here."

He held up the snapshot. "Is that you, Mr. Dodson?"

"Yeah. That's me. But how did you get my picture?" Suddenly Dodson was obviously shaken.

"It's not the first time you've had your picture taken."

Weachter was bluffing. At the time all he knew was that Dodson was a suspect in the Kline case. He hadn't seen his rap sheet, didn't know his sordid history.

Dodson didn't reply, but he seemed to wilt. His confidence was weakened. Weachter read him his rights.

But the trooper's problems weren't over. When he radioed headquarters, he was told that there was no one available to come and assist him in removing Dodson and the fuel truck. Multiple accidents throughout the county had every trooper on duty.

"I'll tell you what I'm going to do," Weachter addressed his prisoner. "I'm going to let you get back in the truck and drive it back to the company terminal. But remember one thing. I'll be right behind you all the way."

Weachter indicated the pistol. One shot could turn the truck into a blazing inferno.

"Sure. I'll be glad to do that," said Dodson. His shark's grin was back. "You'll find out you got the wrong guy. I never touched that woman."

Another trooper met them at the company terminal in St. Thomas as the closely escorted fuel truck was backed into place. Weachter was glad to have company. He handcuffed Dodson and put him in the back of the cruiser.

"I'm going in to have a word with your boss," he said. "Officer Wollyung here will keep you company."

"I have something to tell you before you go in there," Dodson said. "There was someone along with me and I guess you'll find out about it. My cousin was riding along with me. I dropped him off at a place and he's waiting there for me now."

Weachter raised his eyebrows. Further corroboration to Lisa Prescott's story.

"But I didn't touch that woman," Dodson insisted.

"Why did you lie? You told me you were alone."

"I didn't want to get my cousin involved."

"That's very kind of you, Mr. Dodson. Why were you returning to her house? You almost stopped your truck at the end of the lane. Then you saw me and kept going. Were you returning to finish the job? Is that why you left your cousin off?"

"No!" But Weachter had struck a nerve. "I was just trying to find the guy who wanted oil delivered. That's the truth." Beads of perspiration appeared on his upper lip and brow.

"I can put the window down if you're hot," offered Wollyung.

"Never mind that," growled Dodson. Handcuffed in the rear seat, he looked caged, his eyes dark with anger.

After notifying Dodson's employer, Weachter and Wollyung drove to the store where Dodson told them he had left his cousin. The cousin came out to the cruiser when he saw Dodson in the back seat.

"Hi, Rich," he said. "What gives?"

"Get in," said Weachter. "We'd like to have a word with you."

The cousin cheerfully obliged. Dodson stared at him sullenly.

"Were you with Mr. Dodson when he stopped at a house near Fort McCord and made a phone call?"

"Yeah. I waited in the truck."

Weachter warned Dodson silently with a look, then continued his questioning.

"How long was he inside the house?"

"I don't know. Quite a while. Then he came out and told me I'd have to wait here at the store for a while. He said he'd be back for me and then we'd go on home."

"Will you come along with us to town? We'd like to talk to you about this. Then we'll see you get home," Weachter told him.

"Sure. I got tired of waiting here in the store," he said. Then, glancing in the rear seat, he stammered, "Why is Richie handcuffed?"

"He might be in a little trouble," said Wollyung.

"Are you going to drive him home too?"

"We'll see," said Weachter as he turned the cruiser toward Chambersburg. The cousins did not speak to each other as

Weachter drove, but he sensed waves of resentment and hatred coming from Dodson.

That afternoon Richard Lee Dodson was charged with attempted rape and committed to the Franklin County Prison in lieu of bond. The cousin was subpoenaed after he willingly gave a written statement. He promised to testify when the matter came up for a hearing.

TWO

A Vision of Fire

Paul Ciprich breathed a sigh of relief when he heard that Dodson had been apprehended. It gave him some valuable time to marshall evidence. And with the suspect behind bars he and Farrell could proceed at a slightly more leisurely pace.

"Let's get a hold of the parole officer," said Farrell. "Tell him we need to know anything and everything about these two gentlemen. From birth to death and in between."

Ciprich promised to get right on it. Farrell had that cold look in his eyes that meant he smelled blood.

"And one more thing," said Farrell, pausing at the door. "We've got to determine which one of them is the weakest. We'll hit him with the first blast. If that doesn't work, we'll try the other one. But first get a complete book on them."

Farrell's tread was heavy as he went down the hall. Ciprich picked up the telephone.

It was nearly noon when Kerry Sanders, the state parole officer, finished his work at the *Record Herald* office. Under his arm a manila folder bulged with clippings on the Kline case, on anything remotely related to the girl's disappearance.

Ken Peiffer passed Sanders at the duplicating machine. He was on his way to lunch when he stopped in his tracks. Sanders was vaguely familiar, but Peiffer couldn't quite place him. He turned back.

"Hi there. How are things going?" he asked.

"OK. You guys sure wrote a lot about the Kline girl," Sanders replied, indicating the folder.

Peiffer's interest soared. What was the guy doing with clippings on Debbie Kline? He found Cox in the dining room, happily devouring a ham and cheese sandwich.

"Do you know anything about this?" he demanded.

"Sure I do. That's Kerry Sanders, the state parole officer. He wanted to see our files on the Kline case. Intriguing, eh?" grinned Cox.

"Damn right. What do we do now? Something's up."

"First thing we do is take a close look at recent arrests, or see if someone just got paroled who has a record somewhere along the line of girl-napping. Maybe the guys at the Chambersburg office can help. They see more of the court stuff than we do," said Cox.

"And let's see if we can squeeze any information out of the local police. If they didn't put anyone on ice, maybe they know who did. Hey! Wait a minute." Peiffer jumped up from the table. He ran back through the office. Cox stared after him, shaking his head.

He was back in a few moments, waving some notes under Cox's nose.

"A light bulb just went on, Bob. Look at this." The headline read, "Attempted Rape Charge Filed."

State police arrested Richard Dodson, 30, of Greencastle, Wednesday, and charged him with attempted rape after an incident near Fort McCord.

Police say Dodson allegedly stopped at the residence of a twenty-six-year-old female one-half-mile north of Fort McCord at about 2 P.M. Wednesday to ask directions.

Once inside the house he allegedly dragged her to a bedroom and detained her there for some time before letting her go.

Police say Dodson was arrested a short time later and charged with attempted rape. He was placed in Franklin County Prison in lieu of $10,000 bond.

Cox whistled. "Did you notice his first name was Richard?" he said.

"Yeah. But what I noticed more was that he had a problem of the kind that goes right along with abducting girls. I think we'd better see what we can find out about this guy," said Peiffer.

It seemed like a long shot.

On January 22, exactly six months to the day after Deborah Sue Kline disappeared, Bob Cox received a phone call from Dorothy Allison.

"Where are you?" a familiar voice accosted him. "Why aren't you here right now? I'm ready to go!"

"My god. Where are you?" a surprised Cox responded.

"I'm over at Ken's place and ready to start. We're both ready. So get yourself on out here and we'll get going."

"I'm on my way," Cox promised.

As he drove over to Peiffer's place, he wondered what to expect. Dorothy Allison was certainly impressive over the phone, and her credentials were quite well documented. But now that she was here, would things "begin to happen" as she had promised? He and Ken had tried to follow up her leads, but there had been nothing concrete to go on. Two first names, very common first names. And the state police had not been cooperative about that fellow Dodson; if he was a suspect, they were keeping it quiet.

It had been six months of frustration, and he hardly dared to hope it was about to end.

Upon entering the Peiffer household he found himself being hugged by an attractive, energetic woman. She was dark, with an olive complexion and boundless energy. It was contagious. Dorothy Allison exuded energy, as though she were a bomb about to explode, or a rocket set to take off.

"You don't need to tell me, Bob," she began. "I know you haven't been able to do anything with the information I gave you over the telephone."

Cox looked at Peiffer. He shrugged and smiled. "No, I didn't tell her."

She was raring to go. "Come on. We're wasting time. Let's hit the road."

Dorothy zipped up an enormous pile-lined parka, complete with fur hood. The jacket dwarfed her, Cox thought.

"I always wear clothes comfortable and warm enough so I don't have to keep thinking of the cold," she explained.

"You're not allowed to read my mind," Cox joked. "I may be thinking things I'd rather keep to myself."

"I wasn't reading your mind. I saw your eyes bug out when you saw this eskimo outfit of mine," she said laughing. It was a spontaneous laugh, the laugh of someone who was determined to get the most out of life, even under the most adverse circumstances.

When they passed through Chambersburg, Dorothy pointed out the Cox residence. "That's where you live, isn't it, Bob? As soon as I saw the bay window, I knew."

Cox lit the wrong end of a filter cigarette. He had never told

Allison where he lived, never described his home. She had driven in from the north, and this was the first time she had ever been to Chambersburg.

The cigarette tasted awful.

"Let's see what we have," bubbled Dorothy, seemingly oblivious to his distress. "I told you their names. By the way, the second one is in jail now, so they won't be going anywhere until we get the goods on them."

Peiffer, distracted by her matter-of-fact tone, nearly ran into a curbstone.

"Turn on the heater, it's cold in here," said a shivering Cox.

"Funny, I was thinking it was too hot," he answered.

"Well, I'm just right," Dorothy threw in.

"By the way," said Peiffer, "Paul Weachter is going to meet us down at Waynesboro Hospital. John Farrell called me last night and said he'd have Weachter there shortly after three."

"Who is Weachter? Does he know about the case?" Dorothy asked.

"He's with the state troopers. I don't think he's on the case, at least he wasn't last week," said Cox. Neither he nor Ken had been made aware of the recent developments at the barracks. Farrell had closed the lid on the subject, preferring to let his men continue their investigation without interference from the press.

"I think I'll like this Weachter. He's the quiet type, isn't he?" said Dorothy.

"You might say that," answered Ken dryly. Weachter's reserve was an outstanding trait.

"You can learn a lot more if you listen," Dorothy commented. "A person already knows what he's going to say. It's better to listen to the other guy."

They were approaching Waynesboro. Both men were silent, watching the psychic, waiting.

"Is there a religious place here?" she asked suddenly. "Like where nuns or novices study?"

"We're not far from Nunnery Road. But the convent has been closed for many years now," said Peiffer.

"Doesn't matter. I go back into the past sometimes. Would Debbie have had occasion to go out that way at any time?"

"I'm sure she did. It's not far from where she lives. She's native to the area, probably traveled that road many times."

Dorothy Allison nodded, staring out the window.

"I wonder if you could possibly have some other religious place in mind," said Cox. "Like Mount St. Mary's or St. Joseph's Provincial House. They're both just a few miles from here. And that's where Elizabeth Seton, the first American saint, spent most of her lifetime."

"That's holy. That's certainly very religious," mused Dorothy. "Something like that is what I mean. As we get near, I seem to pick up things like that. Could she ever have been there?"

"Probably anyone who lives in the area would have been out that way. The shrine and the old-world architecture make it a tourist attraction."

"I may want to go out that way before I go home. We'll see."

When they pulled into the hospital parking lot, Dorothy pointed to a set of doors.

"That's where she came out. It was hot here that day."

She was right on both counts. Paul Weachter was waiting for them. Cox was wondering just what the trooper's reaction would be to the psychic. Weachter, quiet as always, was very polite. As the day wore on, he and the psychic would become friends.

Dorothy toured the hospital, trying to pick up "pictures." Cox was reminded of a bloodhound being primed with the scent. They were joined in the parking lot by three other men in a four-wheel-drive vehicle. All three were friends of the Klines and had volunteered to come along. At Dorothy's insistence she and Cox rode in the police cruiser with Weachter. They headed for the Moyer place.

"We'll have to follow Ken out there," said Weachter. "I've never been there."

"Doesn't matter. Neither have I," said Dorothy. "Maybe we'll pick up some fresh ideas as we go along."

"About that religious feeling you have, Dorothy. I just remembered that the Moyer place, where we're heading now, was last owned by a preacher. It burned down shortly before Debbie disappeared."

"When I talked to you on the telephone, I mentioned fire," said Dorothy. "But the way I see it, fire is very important to one of the men who took her."

Weachter tried not to flinch. Just that morning he'd been checking into the Illinois fire that claimed the lives of Dodson's wife and three children.

"Did they tell you that both of these men are already locked up?" Dorothy asked him. "They're both in jail now."

Weachter kept his eyes on the road. The psychic certainly seemed to be getting right to the point. He wondered what else she knew, wondered whether she would be able to supply him with information that would make Dodson crack.

"She's dead," said Dorothy. "We can't tell the parents yet. That wouldn't be fair until we actually locate the body. But she's been dead since the day they took her."

This time the trooper did flinch, but neither Cox nor Dorothy noticed.

"Oh," he said casually. "You know that much already?"

"Yes. I've known if for quite a while. I told Bob and Ken and made them promise not to tell her parents."

Weachter's eye caught Cox's in the rearview mirror.

"It's true. She told us that before Christmas."

Weachter slowed the cruiser as they approached the ruins of the Moyer property. Dorothy was silent, studying, her mind open.

"Right there is where her car was found," said Cox. Peiffer's car and the four-wheel-drive vehicle pulled in behind them. Dorothy got out and surveyed the scene. The lonely chimney looked as forlorn as ever. The place made Cox uneasy—it had ever since that day in July when he first peered into the flooded cellar.

"The body is not here," said Dorothy. "They took her and left."

The men waited, hands in their pockets, shivering in the cold January air.

"Where do you grow wheat around here?" she asked.

"Mostly west of Conocheague Creek, west of here. Mainly the northwest part of the county."

Dorothy nodded. "I'd search there for the body. It isn't around here."

The caravan left the Moyer property behind. They followed Dorothy Allison's signals that came from her flickering "pictures." In a strange, staccato fashion she would deliver the images. In her mind place and time and compass direction were often transposed or mixed together. She kept receiving the pictures as they circled the area, trying to ascertain where the signal was strongest.

"I don't know how to go north or south," she explained. "I see a place where wheat is grown."

"Does it have to be wheat?" asked Cox. "Could it be something like alfalfa?"

"Wheat," Dorothy insisted. Then after a few minutes, "Something with gold. Like jewelry. A gold ring? I mentioned that on the telephone, I think. I'm not sure what it means, I just feel it."

As he drove, Weachter watched her out of the corner of his eye. Could she read his mind? Did she know what he knew about the recent developments in the case? Weachter considered himself to be a reasonable man, open-minded, but he wasn't sure he was willing to accept the psychic's predictions at face value. Wait and see, he cautioned himself, wait and see.

"I'll tell you what else they do . . . no—it's the way they went, the way they drove after they took the poor girl. Something with medical instruments. Precise instruments. They went in that direction. Do you know where that might be?"

"The only place I can think of is up at Mercersburg. There's a place where delicate medical instruments are cleaned by ultrasonic sound," said Cox.

"How far is that from the hospital?"

"Go that way. It may not be that far, but I think that's the direction," she assured them.

Weachter pulled off to the side of the road to instruct the cars following, and Peiffer joined them in the cruiser. Cox explained the direction they would take.

"But why northwest?" he asked.

"Because that is where I think they took the girl, then raped her and killed her," said Dorothy firmly.

Weachter's stomach was in a turmoil. He knew Fayetteville was where Barbara had told Ciprich the body was buried, and Fayetteville was northeast, not northwest. Yet Dorothy Allison spoke with authority. He thought it best not to interfere, and he dared not tip his hand to the reporters.

They drove northwest.

"I went from one place to another. I'm not in the same town I started in, I know that." Dorothy had begun to speak in the first person, as though she were Debbie. No one else spoke. "As far as the distance goes, it's not clear. But I went to another place."

They drove on.

"What place has an *a* and an *e* in it?" she asked.

"Greencastle . . . Lemasters," thought Peiffer. He closed his eyes, trying to imagine likely names.

"Both are near Mercersburg, where that medical business is located," said Cox.

But Dorothy seemed to ignore the answers. She was receiving other pictures.

"As I talk about it, I get the feeling of sharp instruments. I hear a sound. I thought it was a voice. A very funny sound I hear." She was jumping from past to present tenses, floating through time. "Yes. Like knives. I'm seeing something like a knife."

The cruiser was eerily silent, except for the whirring of Cox's tape recorder.

"It will come to me. Just drive by it and see what happens to me. I will know when we're going in the right direction, and I can tell when we're going away from it. As I said, I may be going from the end to the beginning. Time gets jumbled up. That's something you people will have to figure out."

Peiffer broke the spell as the cruiser passed the Washington Township Municipal Building.

"Dorothy, you said something once to me over the telephone about a carnival and new construction. That township building is brand new, and another addition was just added. And in the field there, beside the building, that's where the carnival was held."

"OK. Good." She perked up, smiling. "If the carnival was here, we should be passing a stream with double letters in it, or someplace with double letters in it."

"On the left is a place called Kress," said Peiffer. "And further down is Good's Dam."

She nodded. "Now, from where this carnival was, where would there be a place with twin bridges?"

After a moment of silence, Peiffer whistled. Weachter was having trouble remaining impassive.

"This is wild," said Peiffer. A long abandoned railroad track, forgotten now by most residents, wound its way through the marshy lowlands about a mile ahead. Weachter pulled over to the side so that Cox could point it out.

"Over there. Can you see those things built in the water? Those are the stone trestles that held up the track, or what's left of them. On the other side of the road is an embankment that was once a railroad bed. But it was abandoned many years ago."

"OK," responded the psychic. "Then we're in the right area.

See, what did I tell you? North, west, south—I don't know. I never want to learn it because it would ruin things. I'd start looking at a map and theorizing. It wouldn't work. I've got to see and know."

Cox recalled his original skepticism about a psychic who didn't know one direction from another.

"There's something bothering me. Something about a line. Or maybe it's a lion. I can't see," she said.

"We're coming up on Lyon Road," said Cox. He was no longer surprised by her eerie ability to "see" something before they came to it. Somehow she made it seem reasonable, natural.

"That might be it, although I didn't think it was a proper name. I get a feeling about a dog, a big dog. A dog that looks almost like a wolf. It isn't Debbie's little dog. I saw that."

She moved around in the seat, picking up energy, opening herself to new sensations. "Check on something like a joint enterprise. It seems like these two guys wanted to get into something together. And where would there be someplace they'd put a trailer camp? On that particular night I see a trailer camp. It may not be many trailers. And I see an old, junky place."

They drove on, a small, grim caravan traveling through an icy landscape.

"Where would they have something that reminds me of a zoo? she asked.

"Over at Catoctin, Maryland. Near Mount St. Mary's College.'

"And where would they have a hospital . . . no, a place where there are insane people?" Dorothy had her eyes closed, her fingertips against her forehead.

"That's nearby. The South Mountain Restoration Center," said Cox. He watched her, trying to imagine what it was she saw in her head.

"Then we're headed in the right direction," she said. A moment later she burst out, "I don't know why, but I get this feeling about a shoe. It's a dark shoe, but that could be because it's dirty.

Remember that. The shoe is very important."

Several days later Weachter would have good reason to recall that particular detail. At that moment, cruising at the psychic's whim, it was just one of her many impressions.

"Is there a place around here, something like a nightclub or a tavern that is referred to as a den?" she asked.

"There are lots of dives around here," Peiffer answered. "There's a place over there that's now called 'The North Forty.' But it changes names pretty often. It might have been called a 'den' at one time. It's just across the state line, in Maryland."

"There's 'line' again! There are lots of lines. The body will be found somewhere near lines—I'm not sure what kind of lines. Where would we find a town where they changed the name and gave it an historic name? It was called by one name, then changed. Something historical. Something in the past."

"There's Mercersburg," said Peiffer. "That's where President James Buchanan was born. It used to be called Black's Town."

"Could it go back a hundred years or so?" asked Cox.

"It doesn't matter," Dorothy replied. "Time doesn't matter."

They had crossed the state line into Maryland and were exploring a network of back roads when Dorothy suggested they might be getting away from where Debbie was taken. She was getting cold. She shivered, adjusting the hood of her parka.

"I feel like we're going away, in the wrong direction. When we crossed those twin bridges—that's as far as we should have gone."

Weachter directed the cruiser north again, back into Pennsylvania.

"I don't know. These crazy people are animals," she said suddenly. A pained expression crossed her face. She had just seen a particularly unpleasant picture. "These crazy people know where to hide somebody. I see a dump."

Then her expression changed and she exclaimed, "Ringgold!"

The three men stared at the roadside posting of Ringgold, Maryland.

"I saw gold and a ring. I don't know—we're getting closer . . ."

Cox spotted something he thought might be relevant. "Did you see that signpost? A big shoe sign. Maybe that's the shoe you were talking about."

But the psychic ignored him, intent on something else. "I'm getting hot again. We must be getting near to something."

She bent her head, her eyes half-closed. After a moment she looked up, eyes widening, as though she had been startled. "This is the whole thing. We must go to a wooded area that we have to walk into."

They waited. The whole area was surrounded by wooded areas. They needed something more. Dorothy continued.

"Those poor souls. Those crazy men. They were animals. We have to find her. Even though she is dead, we must find her. Just to do that will be important. What hell on earth it must be for her parents, not knowing."

There were tears in her eyes, but she quickly wiped them away with the bulky sleeve of her parka.

"The direction she's in. It's a high place. If I had binoculars, I could see a school from there. She's halfway in and halfway out —not completely buried. Not deep."

"And she was a virgin," she added, shaking her head. Watching her, Cox was thankful that he could not see the same disturbing "pictures" that the psychic was seeing. He shivered.

"She might have been burned. They—I see fire . . ." but she didn't finish.

"You keep going back to 'they,' " said Cox after a few moments.

"Because there are two of them. I feel fire, like they burned her, or something burned where she was buried later. Fire is important to these guys. She may have been alive when they left her, just barely. It's as though she was unconscious, in a dream. Fire . . . fire is very important."

And then she burst out, "They were animals!"

"And this guy—both of them are in jail right now. One is a police informer, or something like that. Or maybe he will become an informer. But he's a lot of baloney. Don't believe anything he tells you. He's got fishy eyes. I don't like him. Not at all."

"Could he be someone local?" asked Weachter. He was remembering the flickering, veiled eyes of the rapist he had arrested.

"I don't know if Debbie knew them or not," said Dorothy. "They were in a hurry to be rid of her. They didn't take time to bury her deep. She's not buried deep enough. And I feel we have to be near a furnace thing. It's in the area where she is."

"You don't think they buried her?" Weachter asked.

"She's not buried deep."

Darkness was falling rapidly as the caravan moved back toward Waynesboro. Weachter suggested that they call it a day and try again in the morning. Cox and Peiffer agreed. The tension of the ride was beginning to exhaust them.

"Fine with me," said Dorothy. "Let's start right after breakfast. I think we're getting close."

They agreed to explore the Lyon estate early the next morning. The location had been suggested by Washington Township police chief Harold Gingrich when he heard that the visiting psychic had come up with a repeating image of "line" or "lion." The Lyon estate, abandoned for some years, was in a remote, wooded area, and it had lately been the object of late-night visits by persons unknown.

It seemed like a good place to start.

THREE

The Second Day

As the two reporters drove toward their rendezvous at the Travel-Lodge Motel, they discussed the previous day's search. Both had been impressed with Dorothy Allison.

"My head spun like a top all night," said Cox. "The experience was unreal. And eerie as hell."

There was no other way to describe the feeling he'd had in her presence once the "pictures" started coming to her. Her face and voice inflection remained unchanged, but there had been an unmistakable sensation of charged energy. Peiffer agreed with his assessment of the famed psychic.

"I know. I know. I was up to the wee hours trying to fit the pieces together. I feel we should be able to reach out and touch these guys. But on the other hand, I can't place them."

Both men were groggy when they entered the motel restaurant. The search party had already assembled and, from the looks of it, dined.

"You're late," said Dorothy cheerfully.

"You boys look like you partied last night," said the usually taciturn Weachter, breaking into a grin.

"Hardly," said Cox. "Are we ready to get the show on the road?"

The same three-vehicle caravan set out for the Lyon property. They drove into a darkly wooded area. The occupants of the car fell silent as they passed down a long lane lined with hundreds of walnut trees. At the end of the dead-end road was a large, four-car garage, once grand, but now grown ramshackled. Several hundred feet beyond was the mansion.

Its white pillars, reaching from porch to roof, were reminiscent of a southern plantation. A snow-covered pathway led to a foot bridge over a small stream, then back over a flagstone walk to the porch steps. Large willows, their melancholy branches bent down under the weight of ice, dominated the landscape.

The place had been abandoned for several years, since the last heir died. Tom MacBride, a longtime friend of the Klines who was also the executor of the estate, had a key to the mansion and was familiar with the extensive grounds. He informed them that the place had become a favorite spot for teenagers to congregate. From litter found at the garage and around the main building, it was obvious that someone, perhaps several people, had been there as recently as the previous night.

They entered the grand building by way of the massive oak door. A spiral staircase swept gracefully up from the main lobby. More litter was found underfoot, and a number of broken bottles. Young lovers had apparently found their way into the main building.

Dorothy stopped in the entranceway, her breath rising like fog up the stairwell.

"There's a connection here somehow," she said. "I'm not

sure if the two men who took her are involved with drugs, drinking, and sex parties that go on here, but there is a connection."

More images came to her. The members of the search party waited as she paused, eyes closed.

"They picked her up to use her. One of them went to the hospital and saw her. He wanted her. He came back with the other man and they took her in their car."

They began to wander through the enormous rooms, hoping something else would trigger her special gift. But she sensed that the body wasn't anywhere on the estate, that her image of "line" or "lion" would have to be discovered elsewhere.

"When I go back home today, I'll make arrangements to go under hypnosis. Then I'll be able to see it clearly. I can be in the car they used, just like she was. I'll be able to get you their license number and take you to where the body can be found."

She shook her head, as though to shake away some grisly picture that had come unbidden into her mind. "It's not deep. I see a lot of drinking going on. He's drinking something—a can of something. One of them is an entertainer, or wants to be. He plays an instrument and sings, or tries to. I see a yellow building, but I don't like the place and I don't like the music. Something is wrong. Something is evil. They're crazy. Crazy. They don't think like we think."

"I think it's something like hillbilly music," she added. "And I see two very weird people. I see lots of twin things. There is some kind of balance. Everything I see in this case is double. I see doubles in their names, in the place where she is buried. And there is some kind of joint effort that these two, Ronald and Richard, did that day. I see doubles in the things they shared. God, even in their wives and daughters."

They had gathered in the kitchen of the mansion. Frost obscured the windowpanes and cast a strange light through the room.

"Tell us again what we'll find when we locate the body," asked Cox.

"As I said, she'll be partially buried. Fire has a connection. Maybe the connection is with one of the men who raped her. I think something to do with fire will break the case wide open."

"How much time elapsed after they abducted her until they killed her?" Cox asked.

"Only a few hours. I'll try to fix the exact time for you when I go under hypnosis. One of the murderers is very rebellious. He is a lot shrewder than you may think. Very shrewd. There is a separation inside of him. Something is wrong—his parents don't want him."

"There is a separation of some kind with the other guy too. Someone in his family died a violent death a couple of years ago. He's the one who could stand up in front of you and lie as beautifully as could be. He lies to suit his own purposes, and just because he likes to. They're animals, both of them. And they have long records. They've been caught for crimes before. But they got away with a lot more than they were caught for."

"What if we gave polygraph tests?" asked Weachter. He had been silently observing the psychic for more than an hour, and the other men turned to him, a little startled when he spoke up.

"I don't believe in them. You can hypnotize yourself and get right out of it. These two people are capable of anything. They could convince themselves before the test and believe in their own lies."

Weachter nodded, trying to make it appear that the question had been casual and purely theoretical.

"Something important happened on January 13. One of them was involved in something then," she said, looking at Weachter.

He thought of the rapist he had arrested that day. He opened his jacket, suddenly warm and uncomfortable.

"Do you think they've done it before, something like this?"

Cox asked. He wanted to press her now that she was envisioning things. She might come up with a clue, something really substantial that would lead them directly to the killers.

"I think one of them has. I know he's done it before. He's raped. That scoundrel, he's raped girls before this. He likes to show women how great he thinks he is. He's cold-blooded. Oh, is he cold-blooded." She paused, shivering, for a moment, then continued, "One of them was in love with his own daughter. There was little love between the mother and the daughter. It was incest."

They began to leave the kitchen, heading for the front of the mansion.

"One of them, the one that raped his daughter, has one leg slightly shorter than the other. He has a drug or alcohol problem. And he's definitely in jail right this minute. Time is a factor. I see a clock . . . or maybe a watch. I don't know what time had to do with it, but it was important to her. Time went slowly for Debbie."

They returned to the lobby. MacBride made a vain attempt to clean up some of the debris. It was beginning to get colder.

"Look for a junk place," Dorothy told Weachter. "There's a dump connected with this. It's important."

Then she asked, "Where is the jail around here?"

"The Franklin County Prison is in Chambersburg," said Cox.

"They may be connected with that jail. They may be coming there, or one of them is there now. Check on an illegitimate child. One of them is connected that way. He has somebody pregnant right now. The bastard would rape his own mother. Let's leave. We're finished here," she said positively.

They drove back toward the Kline residence. Dorothy wanted to visit with the family before returning to New Jersey, where, she said, she would immediately make arrangements to go under hypnosis. In the trance state she could travel the same route as Debbie had on that summer day.

En route, Cox asked if they had time to take her on a tour of the northwest part of the county.

"It would be worth it. I feel that. But I must get back home. You'll want to go out that way when I come back next week," she said. Suddenly, as though it had just occurred to her, she asked, "Are there any foreign people around here? People who speak differently?"

"Could you mean migrant laborers?" Cox asked.

"Yes. Sure."

"Lots of them come in, especially fall and summer, to work on the orchards and farms."

"That's it," she said. "I get some kind of connection. I want to go to a junkyard."

"There are lots of junkyards and dumps all over the county," Weachter replied. In fact he had recently glanced at a map pinpointing myriad locations.

"It's weird. I'll want to see some junkyards next week. I feel she can't breathe. I think she died of some kind of suffocation, as if she was unable to breathe right. Something to do with her lungs."

"We'll take the Furnace Road back to the Klines," said Peiffer idly.

"What did you say?" Dorothy was excited. "Furnace. Fire again. There's a lot to do with fire. One of them is obsessed with fire. Is there a park near here? I see a lot of trees. It's near something where you would have recreation for kids. And the color yellow is strong in my mind too, as if Debbie saw something yellow."

As they drove past South Mountain, Dorothy exclaimed, "Was there a kid lost around here sometime ago? Close by I feel there was a hunt for a kid."

Weachter asked her if she thought it was a girl.

"No. A boy. An eleven-year-old boy," she replied.

"Up there, on that mountain, we had an eleven-year-old boy lost about a year ago. A search party found him late that night," Weachter replied. The police officer was stunned. And impressed.

"And about two years ago, there was an eleven-year-old boy lost just over the mountains that way," said Peiffer. "He was never found."

"Doubles," said Dorothy. "Doubles everywhere."

As they drove on, nearing the Kline residence, she continued to receive "pictures."

"There is something to do with employment. Maybe somebody was looking for work. And there is a line. I see a line very strong now. It's important. The body will be found near a line of some kind. And I feel something else important has happened near where her body is. Something you don't remember now, but it will come to you. It will put you on the right road, literally."

Cox and Peiffer exchanged glances. They could use something that would put them on the right road. Dorothy Allison's "pictures" were tantalizing, so tantalizing—but they seemed unable to put it all together. Something vital was missing.

"Where would you see plastic?" she asked. "And swimming pools. I get the feeling of plastic and swimming pools. You must remember everything I tell you. It's all important. And I get the feeling of yellow. It stands out where you can see it. Like a sign."

Then suddenly, "The pool! I'm getting hot now. Something is making me awfully hot!"

Her voice was shaking as she pulled off her parka.

"My god, she's fogging up the window," said Cox.

The window next to her had steamed up. Beads of sweat formed on her forehead.

"My temperature is up to about two thousand degrees. I'm so hot I'm burning. That's what I feel about the girl right now. Remember what I said about a plastic swimming pool."

Cox cracked open a window. He stared at the psychic. Waves of heat seemed to be radiating from her. It was unreal, otherworldly.

"I just saw the shoes!" she cried. "One is muddy, but the other isn't. You'll find broken glass around her. I get the feeling of broken glass, a lot of it. Shattered glass. They had to do something to her so she wouldn't squeal on them. You men may not see some of these things right away, but you will soon. Very soon."

She turned to Weachter, whose poker face revealed nothing of his feelings.

"There is something about a house burning down. There is something about a knifing. You will get that at 9:20 tomorrow or the next day."

He nodded, as though he were accustomed to receiving such exotic information.

"And the void of the moon tonight has something to do with a happening at the jail. Something will happen at the jail today. An escape."

"But at 9:20 one day this week, something good is going to happen on this case. If I wanted to know a secret I didn't know, I would start at 7:30 and keep trying. But 9:20 will be the best time for you to find out anything. You have two hours either way, from 7:30 to 11:30." She seemed to be directing this information toward the trooper.

"And let me tell you something. He will sing like a canary. You'll get your confession. Mark my words."

At the time it sounded like the oddest kind of shorthand, as though she were telling them only half of an equation. But Dorothy was off and flying. She could hardly get the words out fast enough as the "pictures" began to come to her in a barrage.

"But today is a very bad day for a policeman. He will have to be careful. Someone will try to escape from jail today. And someone could get hurt if he isn't careful."

"But with Debbie—I see this. They went from where they

abandoned her car to a different place, to a town with doubles in the name. More hilly than it is here. I don't know why, but I see pines. The word *pines.*"

She turned to Weachter. "You have a picture of one of the guys who did it. I would dig into their love lives, because you'll find a lot there, something to make them crack. You've got to get this one guy at a good time so you can nab him forever. He's an animal. He'd do it again. But he'll sing just beautifully for you."

Weachter did not reply. He still had Dodson's picture in his pocket.

Dorothy Allison, with Weatcher and Cox, visited with the Klines for half an hour. The Klines had not been told that Dorothy was positive that their daughter was dead, and they all felt uncomfortable, a little guilty that they had spent most of the day looking for Debbie's body. Much was unspoken between the searchers and the parents of the missing girl, but Jane Kline did not need an explanation of their woeful expressions.

She knew.

Weachter and Cox returned Dorothy to her motel. She had just enough time to pack and leave before night fell. Before they left she decided to erase the lingering doubt she knew existed in the mind of the quiet state trooper.

"*Your* little girl," she asked Weachter, "What time of day was she born? Was there any trouble with the birth?"

"She was born early in the morning," replied Weachter. "And no, there wasn't any trouble. It was a normal birth."

"You're wrong. The child was born in the afternoon, and the doctor had to turn the baby before it could be born," she stated.

She had a faraway look in her eye, and just the slightest trace of amusement showed in her lips.

"No," said Weachter, adamantly. "I remember it very well. I was on duty at the time, but I remember exactly what happened."

"Call your wife. I don't think I'm wrong," said Dorothy.

Weachter hurried into the motel lobby. His stride indicated the irritation he felt. He didn't begrudge the accuracy of her predictions and visions concerning the Kline case, but the psychic had a lot of nerve correcting him about the circumstance of his own daughter's birth.

When he returned a few minutes later, he looked both sheepish and flabbergasted.

"She was born in the afternoon, as you said," he said. "And she was facing the wrong way. The doctor turned her before delivery. My wife never told me because she didn't want me to worry about it." Peiffer and Cox looked at each other incredulously.

Dorothy Allison left Cox, Peiffer, and Weachter with eight hours of tapes. They stopped at the *Record Herald* offices and spent several hours going over the recordings. Weachter made notes, but he kept his own counsel: He didn't want to let the reporters know just how pertinent some of the psychic's impressions were. John Farrell had given him orders—lips sealed until the case was closed—and although the trooper was friendly with both Cox and Peiffer, he knew that their first allegiance was to the press, as his was to the force.

And so the reporters continued to labor in ignorance, captivated by the psychic's impressions, but they were somehow no closer to the truth. They were ready to break up and go their separate ways when the police monitor caught their attention.

State police were being summoned to the Franklin County Detention Center. A breakout had been attempted.

"I don't believe it!" Peiffer moaned. "Someone has got to be putting us on!"

Weachter had put on his coat and was moving through the office when the dispatcher repeated the message.

"What's all the fuss," he asked innocently.

"It's the prison break she predicted. It's happening right now!" exclaimed Cox. Weachter rushed out, shaking his head in disbelief. The two reporters followed him out the door. The initial excitement of the day's activities had returned. They had been touched once more by the ghostly imprint of Dorothy Allison's astonishing energy—and this time just hours after she had left.

"We'd better save those tapes," said Cox. "If she can predict something as unlikely as that, who knows what the rest of what she saw will bring?"

Peiffer was deep in thought as he warmed up the car. "I wonder," he mused, "if it means anything that she showed up six months to the day that Debbie disappeared? It's just uncanny."

Activity at the detention center was nearly back to normal by the time the men arrived. Sheriff Frank Bender gave them the story.

"A sixteen-year-old boy grabbed a matron and tried to choke her. He's a big kid—over six feet tall and about two hundred pounds. He wanted the keys. Luckily another guard missed her and found them. He managed to break the boy's grip. We've removed him to the prison until he can be arraigned on a charge of attempted prison break and assault of a law officer."

"When exactly did this happen?" Cox asked.

"About 4:50 P.M., as near as we can figure. Why do you ask?"

Cox looked at his watch and then said, "We knew about it

at 1:30 this afternoon. I guess we should have called you."

"What the hell is that supposed to mean?" asked the sheriff. He did not relish being put on by members of the press.

Both reporters grinned. "You'd never believe it."

As they filed out of the detention center, they were both laughing.

"You get the feeling Frank Bender thinks we're a couple of flakes?" asked Cox.

"He probably thinks we're high on something," replied Peiffer.

"In a way he's right. I'm about as high as I want to get, ever," said Cox. "Hey! I wonder where Weachter went. I expected to find him here."

"Beats me, Bob. He's probably at home taking a cold shower. It's hard to tell with Weachter, but I think Allison got to him. He was pretty damned surprised when she came up with that stuff about his daughter."

In fact, Weachter had returned to the Chambersburg barracks. He wanted to have his notes in shape for his morning conference with Farrell. Weachter was not inclined to jump to conclusions, but he thought he might have something to hit Dodson with.

Fire.

FOUR

Another Break

  Franklin County was buzzing with the news. The publicity generated by Dorothy Allison's appearance had stimulated a resurgence of interest in the disappearance of Debbie Kline.
  One article detailed her previous accomplishments: her spectacular success in finding missing persons and fingering criminals. Another stressed that she would soon be undergoing hypnosis. Mrs. Allison was quoted as saying she would be able to pinpoint the exact location where the girl could be found, as well as the license-plate numbers of the abductor's car.
  The *Record Herald* was swamped with calls.
  One elderly man offered to accompany the psychic to the hypnotist's office.
  "Sure thing, young fella," he said to the astonished Peiffer. "Just put me under the spell, like that lady from New Jersey, and

maybe I got some secrets in my head too. After all, I lived here all my life."

The rumors were circulating at the Franklin County prison. The psychic had already predicted the breakout attempt, and she had vowed to return and name the abductors of Debbie Kline. She had done it before, the superstitious prisoners were saying, and she would do it again. She even claimed to know the names of the two criminals, although the *Record Herald* had declined to print that information pending further investigation by the state police.

Richard Dodson seemed curiously unaffected by the rumors.

"They think they know about it," he muttered to his cellmate. "But they don't. Not a goddamn thing. It's a lot of hogwash, all this stuff in the papers. It's a big bluff. Do you hear me? A bluff!"

And he shook his fist in the face of his astonished cellmate.

Paul Ciprich was off duty when the call came in from Central Junior High School. The time was 9:20 A.M., duly noted by Weachter. The principal of the school wanted to talk to the investigator in charge of the Kline case, and with Ciprich out the call was transferred to Corporal Farrell.

It seemed that one of the students had something to say about the case. She was ill and with the school nurse, but she insisted she must talk to the authorities.

"Let's go," Farrell said to Weachter. "More dirt on the Kline disappearance."

A heavy snowstorm had moved over the county, and the roads were thick with it. Farrell looked like an immense snowman as he stomped into the principal's office. He was not the least surprised to see that the would-be informant was Candy Jo Henninger. The nurse explained that the girl might be pregnant, that her illness could have been caused by morning sickness.

Apparently the threat of pregnancy had terrified the girl and hardened her even more against the man responsible.

"I think I know who kidnapped Debbie Kline," she said. "It was my stepfather, Ron Henninger, and his friend Richie Dodson."

"Tell us about it," said Farrell as he took a seat next to the girl. "How do you know about this?"

"Well, it's a long story, but here goes," Candy Jo smiled weakly. She had one hand on her abdomen and seemed to be in some distress. "Last summer, after I heard about her being missing, I heard my mother and Ron talking about it in their bedroom. We live in a trailer and the walls are thin, so I could hear most of what they were saying."

"Then a couple of days later Ron raped me. I already told about that. He skipped out before you guys could catch him. Then after that Rich Dodson moved in with mom and I heard them talking about it too," said Candy Jo. She looked younger and younger as she talked, as though she were shedding an assumed worldliness.

"It was Richard who told my mother most of it. It was bothering him so he couldn't sleep. I heard him crying about it to my mother. He told her how Debbie looked, about the blood and all. He said my stepfather killed her and they threw her body on a dump somewhere."

"It's been bothering me so much I been seeing it in my sleep. I just *had* to tell someone about it." She broke down, tears pouring down her cheeks. Farrell summoned the nurse and he and Weachter left.

"I want to hear this from Barbara Henninger with my own ears," said Farrell. The interview had bothered him and he wanted to redouble his efforts to wrap up the case. He still needed an angle —something that would pry a confession out of Dodson. But the man was a hardened criminal and probably knew enough about the law to realize that all they had was hearsay evidence, most of it inadmissible in court. Maybe Henninger's wife could help them out.

Farrell was preoccupied as he barreled the cruiser around the slippery curves, and Weachter knew better than to speak up.

Barbara Henninger permitted them to enter the trailer. She sounded resigned, as though she had been expecting them.

"I told it all to Paul Ciprich," she said.

"Tell it again," directed Farrell.

She went over everything once more, and then she added what seemed to be the incident that had triggered Dodson to open up to her.

"One time he took me out in the car. We had driven to the top of Eagle Rock. He became very emotional up there, and that's the first time he ever told me about the Kline girl. That's when he said she was dead, and that Ronald had killed her."

"I suppose it must have been something about the surroundings. The mountains and all the trees and being at the very top, looking over the valley—I don't really know."

"Did you discuss it when you got back home?" asked Weachter. The walls of the tiny trailer seemed to be pressing in on them. The space heater made the air stifling, and Weachter wanted to conclude the interview and get out.

"Yes, we did. He got emotional all over again, crying and everything. That's probably when Candy Jo first overheard it. After that he used to talk about it all the time. He had what they call a fixation or something. It really bugged him. He said he thought he might be losing his mind. I even went with him to a doctor and got him some medicine to make him sleep. Of course he didn't let on to the doctor *why* he couldn't sleep."

"Can you tell us anything else?" asked Farrell, still pushing for an angle.

"Well, there was one thing that bothered him," Barbara fidgeted, hesitating. "His wife and three of his kids burned up in a fire out in Illinois. I think both things were working on him and he had to let it out to someone. I happened to be there."

"Will you testify against them if we get them to trial?" asked Weachter.

"I can't. I'm still married to Ronald," she stated flatly, as though she had anticipated the question.

"Did you ever think of getting a divorce? He raped your daughter, and it looks like he raped and murdered at least one other girl," said Farrell. He stared at Barbara Henninger as though she were from another planet, an exotic creature he could not possibly comprehend.

"Sure. Sure, I want to," she said defensively. "But I don't have the money for that."

"Try Social Services. They handle indigent cases," said Weachter.

He stood up to leave. Farrell followed, shaking his head as they trooped back through the snowdrifts to the cruiser.

"I think we should hit him with it now. He's ripe for the taking," said Weachter. He and Farrell were back at the barracks, drinking hot coffee in the lunchroom. It was an environment familiar to both of them, and the relief from the tension made Weachter more talkative than usual.

"Could be. But let's kick it around first. I think you're right. If there's a weak spot, it's Dodson," said Farrell. "What do you know about the fire that wiped out his family?"

"As much as anyone but Dodson, I guess. Something stinks about it," said Weachter. "He told me about it the night I busted him for attempted rape up at Fort McCord. He kept changing the story, seemingly trying to hide it, or hide something from himself maybe. He said it had him all mixed up, but what seemed to bother him most was that they went ahead and sentenced him two days after it happened."

"Did he have anything to do with the fire?" Even John Farrell, who had seen all kinds of horrible things in his years on the force, had trouble imagining the type of man who would burn up his own family in order to gain sympathy from a court. It was inconceivable.

"There's no evidence he did. They had an investigation, but it was inconclusive. He must feel guilty about something though. Maybe because he didn't try to pull them out. Or maybe something worse. The first time he told me about it I assumed he wasn't around when the fire started. Then later he admitted he was in the house. He got out without a scratch, and his wife and kids went up in smoke. I don't believe it. You know, if it had been me or any other father, I know . . ."

Farrell nodded. He tapped his fingers on the table, considering the various implications before he spoke. "Okay. That's it. That's where we hit him. It's got to be his weak spot."

"I agree," said Weachter. He didn't bother to add that Dorothy Allison also agreed. John Farrell had little use for psychics. He knew what sort of evidence was admissible, what was needed in order to convict a man of murder, and he intended to go right by the book.

"Let's see if we can get something that will make him break," said Weachter. "Something that will tie in Debbie Kline with his wife and kids."

Farrell agreed. Neither of them could muster up an ounce of sympathy for Richard Dodson. Not when they thought about what Dorothy had felt had happened to Debbie.

The two state troopers decided to pay a visit to Jane and Dick Kline. When they arrived at the Klines, they were greeted with trepidation. Jane had resigned herself to receiving bad news. Dorothy Allison had not told them that she knew their daughter was dead, but the implication had certainly been there. Jane was prepared to accept the inevitable: It was the constant waiting, the never-quite-knowing that she could barely endure.

Weachter explained what they were after.

"We have a suspect. He's in jail now for another crime and we want to question him."

John Farrell was nervously studying the floor. Death was heavy in the air, as though Debbie Kline herself was the girl about to reach out and touch her parents from the grave.

Jane Kline silently handed him two pictures. One was large, a recent photo of Debbie in her graduation gown. The other was a snapshot of Debbie at the age of seven. Perfect, thought Weachter. One of Dodson's daughters had been just that age.

He and Farrell returned to the barracks convinced that they were about to crack the case. It was late. They'd taken leave of the Klines at nearly 11 P.M., and the barracks were deserted, except for the night desk.

"Do you think Hussack will go along with this?" asked Weachter, indicating the photographs. Sergeant Raymond Hussack was their superior officer. They would need to clear it with him before questioning Dodson.

"I know he will," Farrell assured him. "He wants to clear up this investigation now more than ever. Before that crazy woman from New Jersey catches us with egg on our faces. Now let's go home. Tomorrow will be a long day."

Tomorrow would be the second longest day of Richard Dodson's life.

FIVE

Final Predictions

Cox received a call from Dorothy Allison at 5 P.M. the same day, just as he was sitting down to dinner.

"I just saw something you ought to know about," she warned. "Within six hours you are going to have more trouble down there with a law-enforcement officer."

"What do you mean?" asked Cox. Her last foreshadowing had been uncanny, and now, once again, he didn't know what to expect from her.

"Remember, keep thinking doubles. What happened before will happen again. Everything I see has double connotations. Everything works in pairs. What happened before will happen again. I see a red brick building. Watch the corners. There could be a knifing."

The detention center was red brick, he knew. Dinner was

getting cold, but suddenly he'd lost his appetite.

"I'm going to Florida tomorrow," continued Dorothy. "Something else has come up. But I'll be back in time to undergo hypnosis on Saturday. Are you and Ken and Paul cleared to be there? I need you all to ask questions while I'm under."

"Don't worry. We'll be there. Nothing could keep us away."

"There's something that could," she suggested, her voice ringing over the line.

"What's that?"

"If Paul Weachter does what I told him to do, there will be no reason for me to come down. He's very close. Are you keeping in touch with him?"

"I'll call him tomorrow," Cox promised. But glumly he reminded himself that Weachter wasn't likely to tell him a thing. Weachter always played it close to the vest, he thought.

"Don't forget!" she cautioned.

Cox picked listlessly at his dinner, glancing at the clock.

At 10:45 that Tuesday night a male inmate attacked a matron as she attempted to transfer him from the second to the first floor. He had threatened to stab her if she didn't cooperate, and when she refused, he struck her in the face.

It was the second attempted prison break in as many days.

"She did it again," said Cox, shaking his head. He and Peiffer had heard the news as soon as they arrived at the *Herald* offices Wednesday morning.

"She's got to knock this off," said Peiffer. "I'm getting afraid to answer the telephone."

Cox nodded. "I know what you mean. By the way, she told me it was important to contact Weachter today."

"I'm in court this morning. I'll see him there," said Peiffer. "I can't wait to jerk his chain about those attempted breaks."

"Don't jerk too hard," cautioned Cox. "It looks like he may be our closest ally on the Kline case."

That same morning Farrell, Ciprich, and Weachter were filing out of Sergeant Hussack's office in a state of nervous anticipation. Hussack had given them the approval needed to confront Dodson at the jail. Ciprich, just back from a day off, was particularly pleased. He had been itching to get at Dodson for some time. He regarded the interview with Candy Jo as icing on the cake, corroborating, as it did, Barbara Henninger's earlier version.

"This guy is due for a fall," he said. "Today."

The three investigators commandeered the "Snoops Room" and set to work reviewing all the information they had gathered on Dodson and Henninger. Practicing all angles, Weachter and Farrell bounced questions off Ciprich, who took the part of the criminal. They had no idea how Dodson would react, and they wanted to be as familiar with his personality as was humanly possible.

Kerry Sanders, the probation officer, had compiled a complete report, including the extensive newspaper clippings on the case. And one additional fact had just come to light: Dodson was illegitimate. The alleged father's name even had double letters in it, Weachter noted. He was beginning to accept the psychic's mysterious powers as a matter of course.

"We need to concentrate on the fire," Weachter reasoned. "His wife was killed. Three of his four children were killed. And Timmy, his little boy, was severely scarred. He's in a burn center in Illinois."

"God almighty," said Ciprich. He had known about the fire, but every time the little boy was mentioned, his skin crawled. He had seen burn victims before.

"It's like this," Farrell said in review. "Dodson pulls a fourteen-year-old girl off her bicycle and rapes her. A year later he's finally up for sentencing. Two days before he's due for the final word, his house burns down and his family is wiped out. Now, we don't have any evidence Dodson set the fire, but I say that we should confront him with it and see if he breaks. That's strictly by the books, gentlemen. I want this to stick in court. Right now we have nothing but hearsay evidence, as you well know. We don't have the body, and we don't have a witness at the scene. We've got to try and get both."

"We're as ready as we'll ever be, I'd say," said Ciprich. Weachter nodded his agreement.

"OK. Go see the bastard, and lots of luck. If he breaks, give a yell and I'll set up anything you need from here," said Farrell.

Late that morning Ciprich and Weachter left for the Franklin County prison.

About 10:30 Peiffer called Cox from the county courtroom. He sounded perturbed.

"Something's up. I was sitting here in court when all of a sudden the state cops disappeared. Right out the door without a word."

"Damn. Did you talk to Weachter?" Cox asked, drumming his fingers nervously on his desk.

"No," replied Peiffer. "And that's what bothers me. He was due to testify on several of the pending cases. I didn't see Ciprich or Farrell either. Any idea what's going on?"

"My gut is doing flip-flops, Ken. Dorothy said there might not be any reason for her to undergo hypnosis this weekend. I think the case is breaking right now and we're still in the dark. We've spent six months on top of this and I'll be damned if I'm going to read about it in some other newspaper. Can you get away from court?"

"You bet. There's nothing happening here. Everything is being continued until next month's session."

"Let's hit the road then. Where can I meet you?"

"At the Fayetteville bypass on U.S. 30," said Peiffer. "And fear not. I've got a hunch on this one."

Ciprich and Weachter were talking to Warden Robert Holland. When they mentioned the Kline case, his eyes lit up and he promised full cooperation. He directed them to the conference room. There would be, he vowed, no interruptions. Dodson, he added, was a pretty tough egg.

"Give us about five minutes before you send him in," said Ciprich. He took a deep breath as they entered the room. The stark walls were not conducive to conversation, but then their little talk with Dodson was not intended to be a social call.

Weachter set up Debbie's picture at one end of the long table. He leaned the snapshot against the larger frame. Both pictures faced the doorway. When Dodson entered, he would be faced with the pictures immediately. They sat down and waited, pulses racing.

There was a knock on the door. Richard Dodson walked in, his thumbs hooked in his pants pockets. He nodded to the two policemen and took a seat at the end of the table.

He glanced cooly at the pictures, then back to Ciprich and Weachter. A damned cold customer, thought Weachter, who had been expecting the pictures to produce some kind of reaction. Ciprich broke the silence.

"Mr. Dodson, I'm about to read you your rights. Then we have some questions."

Dodson looked up at the ceiling, implying that he couldn't care less. His hands were clasped before him. After the legal formality was completed, Ciprich asked if he wished his lawyer to be present.

"A public defender has been appointed to represent you on the rape charge. We can get him for you if you want."

"What the hell for? I haven't done anything. And I didn't rape that bitch. She's lying." Dodson scratched his chest and yawned, directing his eerie smile at the officers.

"We want to talk to you about Debbie Kline," said Weachter quietly. He felt something gathering in the air, a static charge of expectation. "We have information that you have knowledge about her disappearance."

"That's a goddamn lie!" Dodson retorted indignantly.

Both officers waited a moment, letting him boil.

"Can you see those pictures?" Weachter asked, pointing to the photographs.

"I can see the big one," Dodson replied. He folded his arms across his chest. His fiery sideburns seemed to crackle with defiance.

"Can you see the little picture?"

"Naw," Dodson replied, disinterested.

Weachter picked up the snapshot and tossed it across the table. It slid to a stop directly in front of Dodson. He picked it up, glanced at it, then casually dropped it from his fingers. He stared boldly at Ciprich, who had maintained silence as Weachter proceeded with the interrogation.

"That's Debbie Kline when she was seven years old. The same age as your little girl when she died in that fire. You killed both of them, didn't you?"

"No!" Dodson shouted. He stood up, his eyes wild.

"Yes, you did. You killed them both. You burned your house down because you thought you would draw a lighter sentence, and you killed Debbie Kline after you raped her," said Weachter, matter-of-factly.

"No! No!" Dodson put his hands to his ears, trying to ward off the accusations.

"Yes. You killed them," repeated Weachter.

"But I didn't want to do it!" Dodson cried out.

Ciprich exhaled sharply. It was out. It was over now, six months of frustration, heartbreak, and sorrow. Dodson was going to confess. He'd taken the first step and he was about to "sing like a canary," just as Dorothy Allison had predicted.

Both officers had assumed they would have to hammer at Dodson, "the tough egg," "the cool customer," for hours. But he had broken within a few minutes. It had happened so fast that they were at a loss as to where to go next. They were both on their feet, silent as the man on the other side of the table collapsed, sobbing, his head cradled in his arms. One blurry tattoo, a pathetic symbol of his strength, showed on Dodson's right bicep.

"My only concern is that Debbie is lying out there without a decent burial," said Weachter.

Dodson looked up, his eyes red, then bowed his head again.

"I won't tell anything else until I talk to a priest," he cried out. "I must have a priest."

"Take us to where you hid the body. Then we'll let you talk to a priest," said Weachter. "We won't ask you anything. Just take us to the body. After you talk to a priest, you can talk to us."

Dodson didn't answer. He kept his head buried in his arms, his shoulders quivering.

"Debbie's parents should know. They've gone through hell. There's no use waiting any longer. They have a right to know, a right to give her a Christian burial," Weachter continued.

Dodson was wilting before their eyes. His broad shoulders seemed visibly narrower. He was trapped and crumbling, and he knew it.

"Just lead us to the body, for god's sake. For her parents' sake. We'll take you to a priest just as soon as you show us where the body is. You don't have to tell us a thing until then," Weachter urged. That would be the final straw, he knew. Dodson's knowledge of the body's whereabouts would be irrefutably damning evidence.

After a long moment of silence, Dodson replied. "OK. I'll take you to her. But I still want a priest."

"Right. I'll see if I can get one," said Weachter. He went for the phone while Ciprich kept an eye on Dodson. He called several of the area parishes. Father Hoke, priest of the Corpus Christi Church, would be available later that afternoon. At the moment he was at a funeral. Another delay—Weachter grimaced as he returned to the conference room. Dodson might change his mind by afternoon.

He fully expected Dodson to refuse, to insist on waiting.

"OK," said Dodson. "I'll take you to the body now. But I want that priest before I make a statement."

Weachter's knees were shaking. Ciprich tossed back his hair and made eye contact. They'd done it! And when Weachter finally got through to Sergeant Hussack, he was exultant.

"We got him!" he shouted. "He's agreed to take us to the body!"

"Where is it?" was Hussack's stern reply.

"My God. I forgot to ask. We'll get a release from the warden and get back to you."

"Never mind. I'll send Farrell out to the prison. And don't use the open frequency when you radio in. I don't want this to become a circus. This guy may back off if too many people get into the act."

Weachter floated back to the conference room. It seemed too easy.

They had arranged for Dodson's release by the time Farrell and another officer, Gary Carter, joined them.

"Where to?" Farrell asked.

"Fannettsburg," Ciprich replied.

"What happened to Fayetteville?" Farrell asked.

Ciprich shrugged. "I guess Barbara misunderstood. It's Fannettesburg."

Part 4

THE ABDUCTION OF DEBBIE KLINE

(The following narrative is based on statements given by Richard Dodson)

ONE

July 22, 1976

They pulled into the parking lot of a small bar in Carlisle, Pennsylvania. Heat rose in waves over the countryside, radiated from the dark ribbon of the road, and glared from the bright hood of their car.

"I've had enough of this," said the driver. He switched off the engine and leaned back in the seat, a thin, dark-haired man, beginning to bald. He might have been in his late thirties.

"Yeah. I could use a cold beer," said his companion. He was younger, perhaps thirty, and wore his blond hair combed back with long, carefully trimmed sideburns.

Blinded by the glare of heat, they hesitated a moment inside the door, waiting for their eyes to adjust to the relative darkness. It was just before noon and there were no other customers, except for one old man slumped at the bar. The bartender looked happy to see them—to see anybody.

"It's quiet right now," said the bartender. "But this place will be hopping in ten or fifteen minutes. Just as soon as the guys get out for lunch."

The two men nodded and ordered beers.

"Where you guys from? Ain't seen you in here before," he said, pushing the mugs toward them. The younger man seemed more disposed toward conversation. His friend stared into his beer.

"Just come from Harrisburg. Looking for work but didn't have no luck."

"Lots of people looking for work these days," said the bartender. He pushed a damp cloth idly around the bar top and glanced at the old man, who was fast asleep.

"Yeah, but up until yesterday, we was both working. We work with a crew pulling house trailers for Rouzerville Fabricators. We got us this crazy boss. Yesterday the guy wants us to hook up the electric service during a thunderstorm. Crazy? Hell, lightning can kill a man like nothing, especially if he's fooling with wiring. We told him to shove it, see, and so he goes and fires the whole crew."

"Hope you find something," said the bartender, assuming an air of professional sympathy. He watched the door, waiting for the lunch crowd.

"My buddy here has a friend in Harrisburg he thought might help us out. But we couldn't find him, so we're heading home again. Hell, I ain't worried none. This guy, our boss—he's always taking spells and firing the whole crew, then calling them back a couple days later."

The place began to fill up, and the bartender moved off to service other customers.

"I ain't going back to that place," said the younger man's

companion. He looked up from his empty mug of beer, his eyes sparkling. "I got better schemes in mind."

"Like what?"

"Just schemes. You'll find out soon enough."

They had another quick beer and grabbed a six-pack to go. The drive became aimless. There had been an unspoken agreement to idle the rest of the day drinking and cruising. As he drank, the older man became more animated, and he dominated the conversation, which centered around work, although both had by now lost all interest in looking for any.

They began to recall past drinking sprees, larks that had sometimes led to sojourns in various jails. The older man bragged about his exploits in the Navy when he had "beat the hell out of that damned Bosun. He should have known better than to mess with me." He and his companion had known each other for more than a year. They had shared a cell together. And they shared women.

The older man began to complain about his wife. He had been married for a short time and already she was getting on his nerves.

"Damn bitch doesn't know when to keep her trap shut. Always butting in, telling me how to run my life. We'll see about that. And that little girl of hers—she's been teasing me. Trying to play grown-up games. I'll fix her wagon, just wait and see." He crushed the beer can and threw it out the window. "Time for another pit stop, wouldn't you say?"

They had come to Hagerstown, Maryland.

The bar was dark and small, but the jukebox was loud and a number of people were gathered around it, including several women. They sat down and ordered beers.

"That one there looks like she wants it," said the younger man, indicating one of the women who was standing at the bar. She was talking and laughing with a couple of men.

"Those pants are so tight it'd take you a week to work them off," he continued.

His friend laughed. "Not me it wouldn't. You want something, you just go after it. You take it."

Intent on proving his point, he got up from his stool and started for the woman, who looked over and smiled. He put his arm around her shoulder and whispered something into her ear. She giggled. He bought her a beer, and when his hand moved down to stroke the tight curve of her buttocks, she did not resist.

The younger man watched them for a few minutes, grinning to himself. He soon lost interest and looked around for something to do. He caught the eye of another woman. She smiled and came over to take the stool his buddy had vacated.

"Your friend there found something to occupy him. Left you all by yourself, has he?" She put out her hand and gently traced the blond outline of his sideburns.

"I guess that's OK by me. I got something to keep me busy, right?"

She nodded and he bought her a drink. As he hustled the woman, inventing stories, he lost sight of his companion. The woman leaned forward, listening to his lies. He had managed to place his hand high up on her thigh, very casually, when his friend returned.

He had a six-pack under each arm, and his eyes were blazing.

"Let's get out of here. Now." He ignored the woman, who stared at him, astonished.

"Sure," said the younger man. He was already half off his stool. He looked at the woman, then back at his companion. He shrugged and moved toward the door.

The woman pouted for a second, then dismissed him with a toss of her head. "See you around, creep."

Outside, after the air-conditioned coolness of the bar, it seemed hotter than ever. They slipped back into the car, wincing at the hot touch of the upholstery. The driver laughed sardonically as he headed the car back toward Waynesboro.

"She was ready, alright," he boasted. "But I wasn't. Not enough meat on her. I like 'em a little more solid. And with a lot more spunk. She was panting so hard it was more fun not giving it to her."

"Hell, you shoulda passed her on to me. That bitch I had was just interested in cadging drinks and swapping lies," complained his passenger.

"Plenty of time left for that. We'll get us something nice."

It was too hot for much conversation. They downed the cold beer quickly and eyed the women they passed, trading obscenities. When they came upon a younger one, the driver would toot the horn and both men would lean out the windows, calling out to her, describing what they would like to do to her. They laughed uproariously at the outraged reactions. One young woman threw a rock at the car, narrowly missing the windshield. They ignored her and drove on.

"We'll stop at 'The North Forty,'" said the older man. "I want to get some information."

They separated soon after entering the bar. The older man approached some men he knew, while his companion looked over the women. He saw nothing to get excited about, but he amused himself bantering with two or three. After a while his friend returned and they left.

"It's still early." The driver glanced at the sun, still lingering in the afternoon sky.

"Yeah. I'm getting pretty restless, if you know what I mean." The younger man rubbed his crotch and laughed.

"Keep it in your pants. I got plans for us." Despite the younger man's pressing, he refused to elaborate. It was not yet five o'clock when they reached Waynesboro.

"We'll drive around for a while," said the older man, assuming a mysterious air. "We'll take in the sights."

His companion spotted a young woman in a shopping-center parking lot and urged his friend to pull in. They cruised slowly up to her.

"Sure would like to take you for a ride," he said, leaning out the window. His shirt sleeves were rolled up, the tattoo on his upper-left bicep proudly displayed. The woman stared at him, surprised. He raised the beer to his lips and looked her over slowly. As his suggestion became pointedly lewd, the startled woman got over her fright.

She began to shout angrily, and the two men wheeled out of the parking lot, laughing with glee.

"Pigs!" she screamed after them.

"No. She ain't the one we want," said the driver, his tone secretive and intimate.

They cruised around for a while, windows down and the radio blasting, before the driver turned abruptly into the Waynesboro Hospital parking lot. It was 5:30 P.M. He switched off the radio.

"It won't be long now," he said. They waited, sipping beer. Suddenly the older man grinned.

"There it is," he said. A young girl in a white pantsuit uniform was walking across the lot. "Nice piece, ain't she?"

The younger man agreed, his excitement building. Something was going to happen at last. They watched as she unlocked her car. When she let down her hair, one of them whistled softly.

They followed her out of the lot. The older man began to mutter softly, describing what he would like to do to the girl. She seemed oblivious to the fact that they were following her.

"You got to learn how to take what you want, kid," said the older man. "You just got to reach out and take it. And don't tell me you never done this before, 'cause I *know* better."

The younger man did not bother to disagree. He was watching the girl intently as she drove, watching her long, honey-colored hair blow back in the breeze. They had left the town behind.

On either side was open farmland. The road was deserted. Only the girl was ahead of them.

"I'm going to pull in front of her up there at the stop sign. When she stops, you go back and get her. Drive her car around behind that burned-out house. You know which one."

"OK. Let's go." His eyes were distant. He saw the hair blowing free and his desire mounted.

The driver tromped on the gas and the Cougar leaped forward.

The car lingered beside her for no more than an instant. Then it surged past, raising gravel. A pebble glanced off the windshield and Debbie flinched. The man was still grinning at her. She could see him out of the corner of her eye as she tried to steer away.

But she had no time to gather her shaken wits. The Cougar's brakes screeched and the car rocked to a halt. It jutted out into the road, cutting her off. She jammed on the brakes, stopping just short of its rear bumper.

Stunned, she stared numbly as a man walked toward her. His gait was unsteady but powerful, swaggering. He was tall and well built, and something metallic was clutched in his fist. Whatever it was caught a point of light as he yanked open the door. She had not thought to lock it.

"Move over."

"But . . . why?" she stammered, uncomprehending.

"Just move over."

His voice was thick and menacing. It was as though he wanted her to fight with him, as though he might relish a struggle. She did as she was told, too shocked to panic. He slid behind the wheel and stepped on the gas, swinging her car around the Cougar. He pulled into the Moyer property. The other car followed.

"Get out."

Fear rose in her throat, vile and sharp, but the toneless urgency of his voice compelled her to obey. The other man got out of the Cougar. Thin strands of greasy hair hung down over his balding forehead. He was still grinning. Debbie shuddered and cried out, "Why?"

But the first man cursed and pushed her toward the Cougar. Her knees wobbled and nearly buckled beneath her. He took hold of her hand and her flesh recoiled.

"Move it," he said harshly. "Get in the back seat. Don't move and keep your mouth shut, hear me?"

The older man watched, unmoving, as she was pushed into the rear seat. The grin on his unshaven face was malevolent. She knew instinctively that they were both from a world other than her own. They lived a life that had never before touched hers.

The two men locked her into the backseat and pushed her Vega along the driveway, down through the mud and into the thick brush. She thought about trying to get out a window, but she knew either of the men could have outrun her, and before she even had a chance to consider the consequences of an attempted escape, they returned.

Her body stiffened as they approached the Cougar. Both men climbed into the front seat, and she breathed a prayer of relief for the respite. The driver looked back at her with cold interest. But the grin was gone and his scrutiny was fleeting. The younger man seemed to be seeking his companion's approval, and he, too, looked straight ahead. Neither spoke.

The Cougar was backed out of the driveway. Debbie looked back, trying to see her car, but it was obscured by an embankment. She hoped it hadn't been damaged. As they proceeded down Gehr Road, some of the numbness left her. She had been going home —she'd been almost there—and now they were taking her further away.

"Why?" she whispered to herself.

There was no answer. The car moved on, passing the cornfields and the herds of cows she saw everyday. The sun was beginning to sink in the sky. Barns stood in dark relief against the fields, golden green, crops swaying slightly in the warm evening breeze.

"Please!" She sat up, trying to get the attention of the two men who were so pointedly ignoring her. "Please! What's going on? Where are you taking me?"

The older man answered gruffly. "Never mind that. Nothing bad is going to happen to you, so just shut up."

His tone of voice was malignant, frightening. The younger man glared at her, his hands clenching. Debbie subsided in despair. Her parents would be coming to the porch to look for her by now. Her mother would already be worried—she was the worrying type, and that was why Debbie always made a point of arriving on time. They were passing houses of people she knew. Biting her lower lip, she looked earnestly for someone she knew. Not a soul was out—no one was relaxing in the last sunshine of the day. They must be having supper, she thought as she frantically searched windows for a face, any face. Someone might look out, see her pass by in a car with two strange men. They might wonder what was going on. Someone would give the alarm.

No one did.

The Cougar made the turn into Waynesboro without passing another car. As they neared the hospital, Debbie's hopes began to quicken. She searched the hospital grounds for a familiar face. No one caught her eye, and she dared not make a motion, for the younger man was staring grimly at her. For the first time she noticed the point of a knife protruding from his clenched fist.

Waynesboro was deserted. The workers had gone home. The shoppers were preparing dinner. Families, like her own family, would be relaxing in their backyards, waiting for the cool of the evening.

"Make sure she don't try nothing," said the driver. He was watching her in the rearview mirror, and Debbie felt his cold eyes pierce her.

She saw a truck approaching. The driver was looking their way idly. But he was looking. Eyeing the two men in the front seat, her heart raced. She made a furtive, frantic gesture with her hand. The truck driver seemed to look more closely at her as he passed by. With all her might she willed him to sense her danger.

See me please. Help me. I'm being kidnapped. I'm trapped. Please help!

Over and over she repeated her silent message. Even after the truck was long out of sight she continued, as though it were a message that could not possibly go unheard.

Now they were clear of Waynesboro, and the road ahead was empty. The car picked up speed and, for an instant, Debbie had an image of her home dwindling in the distance, her family growing smaller and smaller, until they were mere specks. The driver leaned forward and switched on the radio. A twangy love song filled the air. Debbie started involuntarily at the sound and the driver asked if she liked country-western music.

"Sometimes," she answered hoarsely. She seemed to have lost control of her vocal chords.

"We're a couple of big-time country singers," he said. And then, to the other man, "Get me a beer."

He twisted around and gestured at Debbie with the can.

"Want one?"

"No," she said.

They shifted back in their seats, staring at the road as the music drifted back. The driver tapped his hands on the wheel. The younger man turned back to her again.

"Where do you work?"

Thick trees lined either side of the road, their green canopies blurring as the Cougar passed by. Debbie had always enjoyed walking in the woods, looking up through the leaves, daydreaming about the patterns the shadows made. She liked walking alone. But now the trees seemed to be hemming her in almost as much as the smell of stale beer. As the trees hurtled past, she longed to see a house—a man mowing the lawn, stopping to wipe his brow and look up as she passed by, her face a signal of fear.

She roused herself as the man spoke again.

"I said where did you work."

"Waynesboro Hospital."

"Hell, you know where she works," said the driver insolently to his companion.

"So what. I wanted to hear her tell me, that's all," he explained. And then again to Debbie, "Are you a nurse?"

"No. I work in the cafeteria."

He took a long pull on his beer as he gazed at her white uniform. His eyes took on a bold, prying aspect. His leisurely inspection was insolent but, curiously, seemed to lack emotion.

"What's your name?" he asked.

"Debbie."

"Yeah? Debbie what?"

The sound of her name on his lips made her weak. She shrank back into the seat, horror churning in her stomach.

"Debbie Kline," she managed, turning her head away from his flat, insistent voice and the calculation of his eyes. The driver was silent. She could see the beads of sweat forming on the bald part of his scalp. The younger man seemed to have given up trying to make conversation. He turned around and stared ahead at the road.

Debbie was left alone with her thoughts and the tinny blare of the radio. The speaking of her name had caused a rush of reality to well up within her. She felt her life vividly, felt the beat of her heart, the motion of breathing—everything else, everything in that car, seemed apart from her, impersonal. The unyielding seat beneath her, the sides of the car, the two men who had taken her, who continued to terrify her—all seemed to be part of one large, uncaring presence that enveloped her.

Suddenly her mother's face swam before her, clearly. The

face was wrinkled with fright. Debbie struggled up from her comforting silence and burst out, "Why!"

The younger man looked around placidly.

"My parents. They'll be worried," she said in a rush. "They were expecting me home long ago. My dad will be out looking for me."

The driver answered her without looking back. His voice was a drone, a cold insinuation that seemed to press her down.

"We won't be gone long."

She subsided back into the seat. Hope flickered again as they neared the outskirts of Greencastle. A figure appeared ahead of them on the side of the road, an old woman with her back toward the car. Debbie fastened her eyes on the aged back, projecting a mental plea, but the old woman plodded along and never turned as they swept by.

The car slowed as they entered Greencastle. The driver wanted no tangle with a traffic cop. Greencastle was quiet. Occupants of the few cars they met were absorbed in their own affairs and paid no heed to the Cougar. And then they were out of Greencastle, on an open, rural road.

Debbie knew that Mercersburg was a few miles ahead. Hope and fear became a blur. She hardly dared to consider that they might turn off onto one of the back roads that wandered through woods and isolated farms. Mercersburg, she was convinced, was her last chance.

The two men continued to drink. The younger one nodded his head in time to the radio. The song was about a cheating lover. Houses began to dot the roadside as they approached the town. The car slowed. Debbie caught her breath and held it—she could see a group of people up ahead. A man, a woman, and a child between them. The three were walking along the right side of the road, facing the Cougar. She would pass them by inches. If only she could—

The driver whirled. She had barely lifted her trembling hand from her lap.

"Don't make a move! Don't you dare," he growled. His companion put his arm over the seat. The knife was in his hand, the blade wavering hypnotically. Debbie froze, the eager look caught on her face dissolved. She was pinned in place by his eyes until the family was far behind them. The driver threw an empty beer can over his shoulder. It bounced off her knee to the floor.

"Did you see what the little bitch was ready to pull?" The blond man jabbed the point of his knife into the headrest and cursed her furiously.

"Lie down on the seat and keep quiet. Don't move until I tell you, and keep your mouth shut if you ever want to use it again."

She lay down, hiding her face with the palm of her hand, trying to imagine that she was somewhere else—anywhere. Through the windows she could see the tops of houses retreating in a blur. After a few minutes the driver told her to sit up again.

They were off the main road.

The terror of the outburst and the flicker of the knife left her drained of hope. She no longer knew where she was. Only the sun on her left told her that they were heading north. A passive numbness began to creep up on her. She tried to will herself away from them. Unwittingly she was preparing herself for the worst by letting her mental sensors click off, one by one, until she felt she had been swathed in a ball of invisible cotton.

They were in a heavily forested area, climbing up a steep incline. A mountain road. The sun was low, beginning to enter its final orange stage before setting, bright in her eyes.

She was jerked back to awareness momentarily when the car stopped.

"We're going back up. I know a place," said the driver. He wheeled the car around and headed back up the mountain. At the top he turned off onto a dirt road.

"This is it."

Debbie held onto the seat as they bounced over ruts, over piles of brush and debris, rusty cans, old plastic bottles, broken bits of household furniture. A garbage dump.

The car stopped.

For several moments all three sat without making a sound. Tension gathered, building with the slow fury of a thundercloud, while the dark-haired man drained his beer. Then in one sudden motion he crumpled the can and broke the silence.

"Let's get this show on the road."

He turned and looked directly into her eyes.

"Strip," he said.

She continued to look straight ahead. The younger man turned to watch, a leer twisting his lips. She didn't move. Time had ceased to move. All else was incidental.

"I said take off your clothes."

She sat motionless, her eyes unblinking. She didn't seem to hear as he barked his command once more, then again. Her body remained rigid.

"Do as you're told and you won't get hurt. You want to get home, don't you?" His voice was low and ugly.

Debbie heard the word "home" and motioned with her hand, as though beginning to undress.

"No." Her voice was weak. Her hand dropped to her lap.

The older man looked at his companion. He signaled him to get out of the car.

"You hold her down."

Debbie was pushed back on the seat, her arms pinned.

"Why? Why me?" She struggled, kicking, as they began to take off her clothes. The older man, his face a mask of hatred, pulled a knife from his boot and began to wave it in her face.

"I don't want no fuss from you. No lip or else. Do what we want and you won't get hurt."

She ceased her struggles and her face went blank.

When they had finished removing her clothes, they backed off. Then one of them held her down. She could barely feel his fingers pressing into her flesh.

"You go first."

Debbie remained motionless throughout the rape. She was retreating into another world—into her own world. When the first man was done, he got out and sat in the front seat while the second man raped her. His breath was hot in her ear—she was most conscious of his breath. When he was done with her, he stood up, stretching himself.

"Awful hot in here," said the younger man.

Debbie sat up. She gathered her clothes and began to dress, her motions mechanical. No one touched her. She hardly knew they were there. This was a nightmare and soon she would be awakened.

"I think I'll get some air. The beer is gettin' to me. I'm kind of woozy," said the younger man.

His companion, sitting behind the wheel, nodded. He jerked his head toward the girl. "Take her with you. Walk her around, but don't let her out of your sight."

He nodded and stumbled forward. "Come on."

She stared at him, uncomprehending.

"Come on. We're going for a walk. Cool off."

"I don't want to," she said. "I want to go home."

"Go!" The older man hit the back of the seat with his fist. Debbie got out of the car. She began to walk toward the road. The man walked with her. She was grateful that he did not touch her. After a few yards he made her turn back. Smoke was rising from a pile of debris.

"Been a lot of burning in this dump," he said. His tone was conversational. She did not reply.

They were a few feet from the Cougar when the other man got out. Debbie turned her head and looked back at the road. The man walked up behind her. He drew back his hand and punched her hard on the jaw. A great numbness exploded around her. She pitched forward and fell to the ground.

The younger man watched nonchalantly as his companion leaned over the girl. He made a sudden motion. When he stood back up, there was a hunting knife in his hand. It had blood on it.

They both watched as the girl tried to stand up. Blood ran from her neck down over the front of her blouse. She clutched her neck and took a few steps toward the younger man, her eyes glazed with shock. She opened her mouth, as though trying to speak. Later she would come to him in his dreams, walking toward him, trying to speak as the blood ran down her blouse.

"Move away from her. Don't get no blood on you!" the older man shouted.

The girl turned and began to stagger toward the road.

"Stop her!"

The younger man went after her. She was moving in slow motion, as though underwater. He gave her a push and she went down. They stood over her, watching, listening to her breath.

"She ain't dying fast enough," said the older man. He bent over her with his knife and with one quick motion severed her jugular vein.

"You wanted to make a quick kill, that's the way to do it," he said. He jammed the knife into the dirt, clearing it of blood.

They waited. The light began to fade from her eyes. They dragged her back into the dump and threw some debris over her. One of them seized a child's plastic swimming pool and laid it over her. They looked around once.

Before leaving the dump they each cracked a beer. Ronald Henninger, in the driver's seat, laughed. He pushed a few strands of hair up over his balding forehead.

"Well, Dodson. Now you know what a cold-blooded bastard I really am," he said.

TWO

White Shoe, Broken Glass

Cox and Peiffer decided on Peiffer's car. It was equipped with a police and fire monitor. They hoped to pick up some conversation between cruisers, some slip of the tongue that would give them an exact location. Both of them were now certain that "it" was finally happening, although neither could guess the exact nature of "it."

"What are you hearing?" Cox asked anxiously.

"Nothing. Not a damn thing. Oh, the usual traffic accidents. But as far as anything else, not one word. It's like somebody has turned the switch off." Peiffer rapped the radio console in frustration.

"The last thing I heard before I left the *Herald* was that two carloads of state cops had just left the prison. They didn't give a destination over the radio. And the dispatcher at the barracks told them to go on the "silent" band. I couldn't monitor them after that."

"I can't believe they'd do this to us!" Peiffer exclaimed.

"Ha!" Cox responded, disgusted.

"Well, we'll have to do it the hard way. Where to?" Peiffer asked.

"Dorothy said something about pines. Let's head up that way." The Pines, a craft center, was east of Fayetteville near the Adams-Franklin county line.

Peiffer put his foot down and the car leaped forward.

Two unmarked cruisers pulled off Burnt Cabins Road at the top of Fannettsburg Mountain. They parked beside a giant yellow road sign that marked the telephone-line right-of-way across the top of the mountain.

About a hundred feet off the road was a dump. Debris poked out of the snow some thirty-five feet below the telegraph line. They were approximately twenty-five miles directly northwest of where Debbie's car had been abandoned.

The officers looked expectantly at Dodson. He nodded.

"This is the place," he said. His voice was toneless, without discernible emotion.

"You stay put," said Farrell. They handcuffed the prisoner to the rear seat and locked the cruiser doors.

The four investigators carefully found their way down the steep incline to the dump. Then they began their grim search. For the better part of an hour they dusted snow off discarded stoves and refrigerators, tipped back television sets to reveal patches of damp earth. They uncovered piles of garbage, trash of every conceivable kind. Broken glass was everywhere. They found nothing.

They trudged back up the incline. Farrell paused to catch his breath before questioning Dodson.

"What gives?" he asked, exhaling clouds of frost in the cold air. The other men stamped their feet, hands clasped, to keep warm.

"I was sure this is the place," said Dodson. His voice was still toneless. "Is there another dump around here someplace?"

Without a word Farrell signaled his men to get back in the cars. He remembered seeing a smaller dump about a half-mile down the mountain toward Fannettsburg.

"That ain't right," said Dodson sullenly. "This ain't the right direction."

"Let's give it a try, shall we?" said Farrell sharply.

They walked Dodson down into the dump. He insisted that it wasn't the right place. Farrell sighed. Ciprich eyed Dodson, wondering if he could be, after all, lying.

"That first place we went was it. I know it was—right at the top of the mountain. We missed and drove on into Burnt Cabins and then turned around and came back. If you take me on into Burnt Cabins, I'll know for sure." Dodson now seemed eager to help them, or perhaps to be done with it at last.

Farrell agreed. He was willing to humor the suspect. He told Ciprich to take Dodson on a tour of Burnt Cabins Road while he and Carter returned to the first dump and continued their search.

They got back in the cruisers and reversed direction at The Pines Tavern, located half-way up the mountain.

Farrell and Carter clambered down the incline again, cursing the snow, and began to unearth more debris. Twenty minutes later Ciprich called down from the roadside.

"Dodson insists this is the right place!"

They kept at it, uncovering more of the mysterious objects that lay hidden beneath the snow. Finally Dodson called down to Farrell.

"Let me come down there and I'll show you right where it is." His voice carried in the still air. Carter shivered, waiting for the prisoner.

They took the cuffs off Dodson and brought him down the slope.

Cox and Peiffer found the Fayetteville dump deserted. Not a police car to be seen. And the police monitor was still silent.

"Damn it," said Peiffer. "Where do we go from here?"

Cox shrugged. "Beats me. I think we ought to get ourselves to the nearest pay phone and call Dorothy."

Peiffer spun the car around and headed back down the dirt road.

Dodson tromped through the snow, tripping over objects buried underfoot. He found the spot he was looking for.

"It should be right here. We covered her with a plastic swimming pool."

"I looked under that," said Carter. "Nothing there but some old deer bones."

"Then somebody must have moved it," Dodson insisted. "Cause that's sure enough what we used."

He circled around, reaching now and again to turn over debris. The four troopers watched him, fascinated. Dodson lifted up a plastic refuse bag. Then he smiled eerily at Carter.

"There she is," he announced. "Right here like I said."

Carter looked. The other troopers were stumbling over to them. Carter shook his head. He couldn't recognize anything in the snow and rubble.

"Christ almighty!" said Dodson. "Can't you see her. Look here. That's her shoe."

And then the shiver began in the base of Carter's spine,

shooting up his back. He saw, as his eyes focused in the white landscape, a white shoe, and above it the pant leg of a white uniform.

"Oh my God," he said, staring at Dodson.

Deborah Sue Kline had been found.

Farrell glanced at the body and slipped the cuffs back on Dodson.

"Take this son of a bitch out of here before I . . ." He released the prisoner, as though the touch of his flesh was revolting.

Ciprich and Weachter each took one of Dodson's arms and climbed up the incline. Once they gained the roadside they turned and looked back at their companions. All four men were ashen. Only Dodson seemed undisturbed by the discovery. His eerie smile was gone, but he showed no remorse, or any emotion at all.

"Go take that bastard to a priest," cried Farrell from the dump. "He's going to need one!"

Cox and Peiffer finally located a roadside telephone. Peiffer placed the call to New Jersey. Dorothy Allison answered on the first ring. Peiffer was interrupted before he had a chance to explain their predicament.

"They have found the body," said Dorothy. "It happened only moments ago. You have to go to the pines and to the line. It's on the mountain."

"But we went to the Pines and to the Adams County line," said Peiffer. Cox had his head inside the booth and was trying to catch the other half of the conversation.

"Is it northwest of where her car was abandoned?" Dorothy asked.

"No. It's northeast," he replied.

"Then that's not the right place. You want to go northwest. Keep working on it. It will come to you. Something else happened there some time ago. I don't know what it was, but you do," she assured them.

They walked back to the car, completely frustrated. Just then the police monitor broke its silence. The barracks dispatcher was directing the mobile crime unit lab operator to get off the turnpike at Fannettsburg.

"Good God!" the reporters exclaimed in unison. They jumped into Peiffer's car.

"The Pines Tavern! Fannettsburg, with double letters. The county line! It's all there," said Cox as the car began to rocket down the road.

Farrell called Sergeant Hussack on the silent band and informed him of their discovery. He requested the coroner and the troop identification unit out of Harrisburg.

"Better send up some floodlights too. It's getting dark, and we'll be here for quite a while."

Farrell and Carter took out the steel tape and began to take measurements for presentation in court. Debbie's body was determined to be 150 feet across the county line, in Huntington.

As Cox and Peiffer headed for Fannettsburg Mountain, more radio messages confirmed it as the location they sought. A state police helicopter was being dispatched to bring in the pathologist. Trooper Joe Claycomb was directed to the foot of the mountain, where he would meet the helicopter. Cox and Peiffer pulled up behind Claycomb just as he turned off his motor.

"Where?" demanded Cox.

Claycomb grinned. "Hey, what took you guys so long? I've been here for almost two seconds." Then he relented and pointed up the mountainside. "Clear to the top, just over the county line."

"Thanks!"

As the two reporters sped by The Pines Tavern, Cox suddenly remembered what was familiar about the place. "Ken, Dorothy told us something important happened around here. Would you believe *Deadly Pursuit?*"

Cox was referring to the book he had written on the Hollenbaugh kidnapping and manhunt, most of which had taken place in the area they were passing through.

"I know, I know," said Peiffer. "I was almost embarrassed to admit it. I should have thought of that before. Oh well, you know what they say about hindsight."

They found Farrell's cruiser at the top of the mountain and screeched in beside it.

"How the hell did you snoops find out?" he asked them.

"A little bird named Dorothy Allison told us," Cox replied, reaching for his notebook.

Farrell shook his head. He'd heard about the psychic. Then Peiffer hit him with a pointed question.

"Did Dodson tell you who was with him?"

"How the hell . . ." Farrell was incredulous.

The shot in the dark had worked. It had been Dodson all along.

Corporal Mentzer went to the Kline house to break the news. Positive identification had not yet been made, but from all indications their daughter had been found.

Before Jane Kline was sedated she and her husband made an effort to thank all those who had helped in the case. Dick Kline was gentlemanly to the end, his face streaked with tears as he greeted the reporters. The big man thanked everyone for their prayers, then silently went upstairs to comfort his wife.

Dodson, in the meantime, was giving a statement to the court stenographer. He denied absolutely any involvement in the murder, although he readily admitted to the kidnapping and rape.

He named Ronald Henninger as the murderer.

Epilogue

The ordeal was not over for the Klines. The bereaved parents had to go to Carlisle Hospital and offer further proof of identification by examining the clothes—the white uniform which had originally attracted Henninger. They were spared the sight of their daughter's mummified body.

Dick Kline met with reporters one last time before making a plea for privacy.

"We can't believe we'll never see Debbie again. It's going to take awhile for it to sink in, I guess. I want to thank the police. From the very beginning they worked their hearts out to help us. And I know they're working even harder now to bring the murderers to justice."

In reference to the psychic, he said, "Dorothy Allison without a doubt had a profound effect on the case. My wife and I sincerely thank her for her help."

The authorities agreed with the Klines. Sergeant Hussack, who had been informed of the details of Dodson's investigation, told Cox he thought Allison had had a definite psychological effect on the investigation, in particular on the suspect himself, who was aware that a psychic had been called in on the case.

Washington Township made Dorothy an honorary member of their police department.

In a curious footnote to the case, which resulted in a piece of final, damning evidence, Lorrie Dodson told Cox and Peiffer that Ron Henninger had removed Debbie's watch before the two men disposed of the body. Henninger then gave the watch to his wife, Barbara.

Responding to this information, a state trooper was dispatched to the Bingaman farm. Barbara had left the watch in the safekeeping of Mrs. Bingaman, who was flustered upon hearing who the watch originally belonged to.

"I had no idea," she told the trooper, her face white. "Barbara gave me the watch to have it repaired, and to tell the truth I'd forgotten all about it."

The trooper took the watch without a word. Time had run out on Debbie, and now it had run out on her two killers.

Debbie Kline was buried on January 30, 1977, at the Green Hill Cemetery in Waynesboro. More than two hundred relatives, friends, and policemen attended the services.

The Reverend Wendall E. Kent eulogized her and called for understanding.

"The memory Debbie leaves us is one of an exceptional young lady, devoted to her home and family and a source of pride and thanksgiving to all those who knew her. Let us cherish these happy memories."

On the second day of February, Dodson repeated the statements he made on the day he led police to her body. His counsel was present.

A warrant for the arrest of Ronald Henninger was issued, who was at that time incarcerated at the Menard Correctional Institute in Illinois. He refused to sign waivers to transfer him to Pennsylvania to face murder charges. A few weeks later the governor of Illinois ordered him so transferred. Henninger then attempted suicide. His superficial wrist wounds were not serious enough to delay his transfer, however, and at the end of May he was returned to Pennsylvania and held without bail.

Henninger's statements coincided with Dodson's with but one exception. He maintained that Dodson was the first to attack Debbie, that the younger man stabbed her repeatedly with a screwdriver.

Legal maneuvers, motions, and petitions on all sides delayed the judicial process. On June 7, 1977, Richard Dodson entered guilty pleas to charges of kidnapping and murdering Debbie Kline. Rape and conspiracy charges were dismissed during the plea bargaining when Dodson agreed to testify against Henninger in order to escape the death penalty.

On July 8, 1977, Richard Dodson was sentenced to life imprisonment for the murder of Debbie Kline.

On October 11, 1977, Ronald Henninger was sentenced to death for murder in the first degree. He has filed but one appeal, that to the Supreme Court of Pennsylvania, an automatic response when a death sentence is passed. This was commuted to life when the state death penalty was declared unconstitutional.

The state penal system, in its wisdom, has seen fit to transfer Henninger to the Fairview State Hospital, an institution for the criminally insane. At this writing, at $175 a day, it has cost the taxpayers of Franklin County in excess of $50,000, with no recourse as to Henninger's stay at the hospital.

Included among the taxpayers are Jane and Dick Kline.

On January 28, 1978, Richard Dodson began a series of costly appeals—costly, that is, to Franklin County taxpayers, for he is still being represented by public defenders. He has filed suit against the Franklin County Prison Board, charging that he was denied medical attention and subjected to poor living conditions while in prison. He has asked for $50,000 in damages.

Dodson has also, with the cooperation of the Public Defender's Office, filed suit against Judge George Eppinger, District Attorney John Walker, and Assistant District Attorney William Cramer for conspiracy to incarcerate him for murder.

The District Attorney has denied allegations that defense counsel informed his office that Dodson was involved in an unrelated murder. This information is considered a violation of confidence.

Dodson is seeking a quarter of a million dollars in damages and their removal from office.

There is no appeal for the Kline family.

About the Authors

ROBERT V. COX has been an investigative reporter for more than nineteen years, primarily covering the police beat in parts of southeastern Pennsylvania and Maryland. He received the Pulitzer Prize for his reporting of a kidnapping at Shade Gap, Pennsylvania, in 1967 which received national attention and which is recounted in his successful book *Deadly Pursuit* published in 1977. He has been honored by both houses of the Pennsylvania Legislature for excellence in his field and has received many awards from service clubs and media peers.

KENNETH L. PEIFFER, JR., is a photojournalist covering the central Pennsylvania beat for more than twenty years. A graduate of several professional photography schools, including Eastman Kodak, he has received numerous awards, including the Associated Press Members' Newsphoto Contest Award.

Senior-class portrait of Deborah Sue Kline.

Driveway site where Debbie's car was abandoned, just to the left of the barrel.

A state police officer dusts Debbie's car for fingerprints.

Updated version of composite of suspect wanted for questioning.

14 – 76

DEPARTMENT HEADQUARTERS
PENNSYLVANIA STATE POLICE
HARRISBURG

AUGUST 4, 1976

MISSING

DOB : 28 NOV. 57
HGT : 64 IN.
WGT : 130 LBS.
HAIR : BROWN
EYES : HAZEL
SSN : 174 – 50 – 3630

DEBORAH SUE KLINE

ADDRESS: RD #5, WAYNESBORO, QUINCY TWP., FRANKLIN CO., PENNA.
INVESTIGATION DISCLOSES THAT SUBJECT WAS LAST SEEN ON THURSDAY, JULY 22, AT 6:35 P.M. WHEN SHE LEFT HER PLACE OF EMPLOYMENT, THE WAYNESBORO HOSPITAL, WHERE SHE WAS EMPLOYED AS A KITCHEN AID WEARING A WHITE PANTSUIT UNIFORM AND WHITE SHOES, SHE WAS ENROUTE TO HER HOME LOCATED FOUR (4) MILES FROM THE HOSPITAL. SUBJECT'S '76 BURGANDY VEGA WAS FOUND ABANDONED APPROXIMATELY ONE (1) MILE FROM HER RESIDENCE ALONG MENTZER GAP ROAD, IN A POSITION WHICH INDICATES AN APPARENT ATTEMPT AT CONCEALMENT. THE KEYS WERE IN THE VEHICLE, THE LEFT WINDOW WAS DOWN AND THE RIGHT DOOR WAS LOCKED. THE SUBJECT'S PURSE CONTAINING HER WALLET, $30.00 IN U.S. CURRENCY, AND PERSONAL PAPERS WAS FOUND IN THE GLOVE COMPARTMENT.

ANY INFORMATION CONCERNING THIS SUBJECT, CONTACT THE FOLLOWING:

| COMMANDING OFFICER
PENNSYLVANIA STATE POLICE
TROOP "H"
P. O. BOX 1343
HARRISBURG, PENNSYLVANIA 17105
Phone: 717 – 234 – 4051 | OR | DIRECTOR
BUREAU OF CRIMINAL INVESTIGATION
PENNSYLVANIA STATE POLICE
DEPARTMENT HEADQUARTERS
HARRISBURG, PENNSYLVANIA 17120
Phone: 717 – 787 – 4810 |

REFER TO INCIDENT NO. H3 – 50911

Missing-person flyer issued by state police to police departments throughout the nation.

Dick and Jane Kline prepare a Christmas stocking for their missing daughter.

Dorothy Allison holds a Patty Hearst T-shirt as proof of her activities while visiting at the home of the Peiffers.

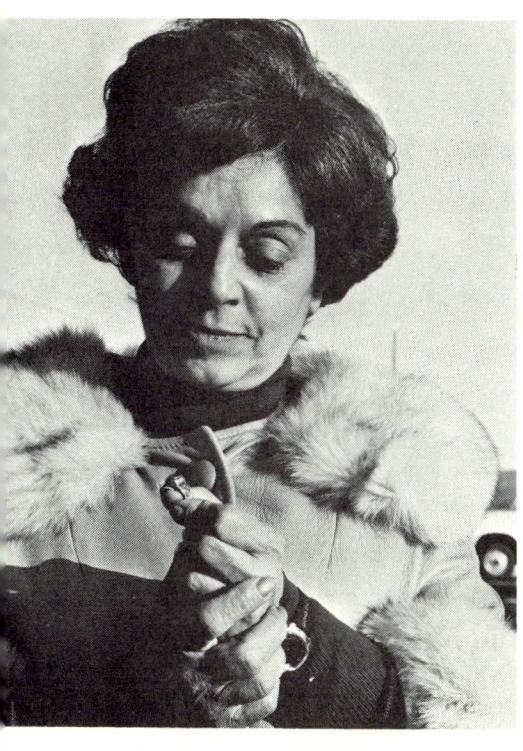

Dorothy Allison concentrates her attention on Debbie's class ring while on a search for the missing girl. January 1976.

Dorothy and Bob Cox trace path Debbie would have taken as she left the Waynesboro Hospital kitchen area in the background.

Dorothy in hooded parka checks a springhouse on the Lyon estate.

Police surround area where Debbie's body was found on a mountaintop trash pile.

Police along with Dr. John P. Manges and Dr. Robert McConagie view Debbie's body.

Richard Dodson sits handcuffed while reading his murder-indictment papers in the office of Justice of the Peace James Campbell.

Ronald Henninger is escorted by Trooper Paul Weachter. Note double reflections, one of Dorothy Allison's predictions.

Relatives and friends gather at graveside during funeral for Debbie.

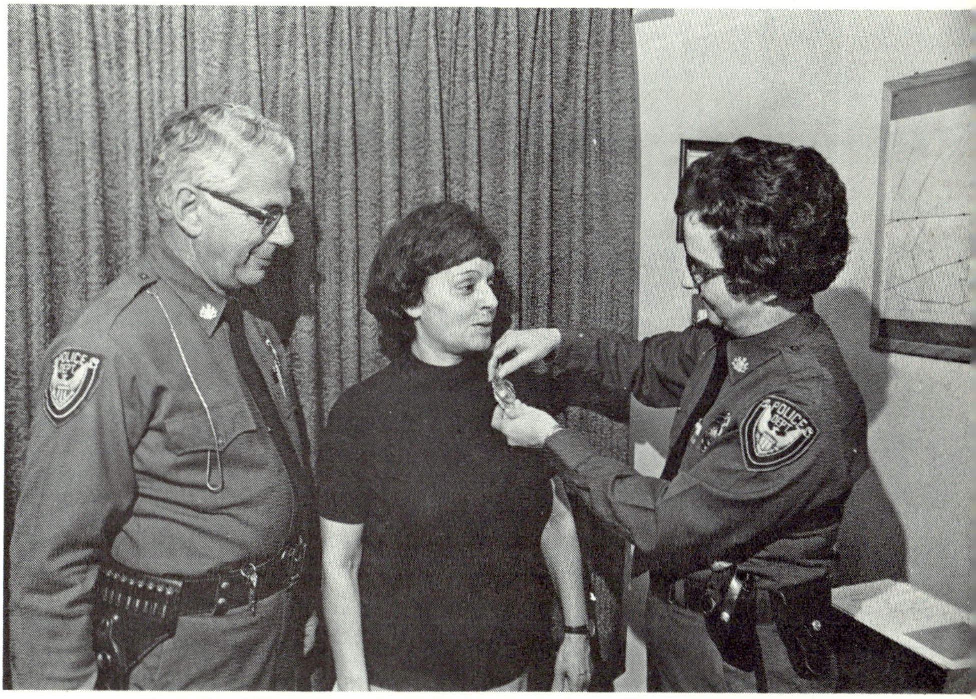

Dorothy Allison is made an honorary police officer of Washington Township by Officer Dorothy Gingrich as Chief Harold Gingrich watches.

Corporal John Farrell leads Henninger to a waiting police cruiser.

Trooper Paul Ciprich, the prime investigator of the Kline case, escorts Richard Dodson, right.

Bob Cox and Ken Peiffer walk the narrow road where the rape and murder of Debbie occurred.